ENDORSEMENTS

Wow! What a book! In my many years of working with Angels in life and ministry, I have discovered that there is always much more to learn—every divine supernatural encounter is intended to bring us into deeper revelation of Christ and His Kingdom—and that is the same result that you will get as you read *Secrets of the Angels*. In reading this book, I felt my mind expanding to receive heavenly counsel and understanding as God's light shone through these pages. My friend Jamie Galloway has written a thought-provoking, eye-opening and prophetically fascinating volume that will lead each reader into a greater awareness of the glory realm! This writing is both biblical and practical. I think everybody should get a copy of this book, which will help further develop their understanding of the Spirit world. Through in-depth examination of the Word, time-tested personal experiences and historical research, Jamie leads us on a journey of receiving fresh revelation for our time. Get ready for your spirit to leap, and your spiritual life to expand, as you journey into discovering the *Secrets of the Angels*.

—Joshua Mills
Co-founder, International Glory Ministries
Bestselling author, *Seeing Angels* and *Angelic Activations*
www.joshuamills.com

Angels and all the heavenly host have always been involved in life on planet earth. However, in these seasons, their activity seems to be on the increase in exponential ways. My friend Jamie Galloway introduces and unveils for us great understanding in their operation. I would encourage this book to be read and enjoyed, as encouragement will fill your soul and replace any fears with a faith in God. You will begin to see all that is working on your behalf.

—Robert Henderson
Best-Selling Author of *The Courts of Heaven* Series

For those supernatural pioneers who are ready to venture to the pool's deep end, take a big breath and plunge into Jamie Galloway's *Secrets of the Angels*. This book contains the historical, biblical, and practical secrets that will help you step into a new level of heavenly activity.

—Darren Stott
Founder of Supernaturalist Ministries, CEO of Renaissance Coalition, and Lead Pastor at Seattle Revival Center

"Angels" is one of those topics that few folks write about, but many have questions about. I was intrigued by the title, and because I know Jamie personally, I knew I wasn't getting something that was akin to a novel with no real-life experience or biblical foundation. I have often wondered why there isn't a larger body of work dealing with this subject because angels and their connection to both mankind and Heaven are very real. In fact, there is a weekly prayer in Jewish liturgy that actually invites these "ministering spirits of God" into the synagogue and home known as "Shalom aleichem." Once you read these pages I am certain you will want to know more about angels and the work they have been assigned by Heaven to accomplish for you!

—Paul Wilbur

My friend Jamie Galloway has gone DEEP on this incredible, insightful, thoughtful, and theologically timely book on angels. The Bible confirms the fact that we are surrounded by invisible realities, where Heaven touches Earth and God's angels intervene and intercede on behalf of human beings. There has been both much ignorance and the imaginary about these celestial beings and their objectives. But what if angels are much more involved in our everyday lives and purposes than we have been taught? What if we can partner to a greater degree with their mission? This book you hold, *Secrets of the Angels*, will give you sound biblical keys and revelation that will help you embrace and enter a new Kingdom dimension of serving and beholding the Lord Jesus Christ.

—Sean Smith
www.seanandchristasmith.com
Author of *Prophetic Evangelism* and *I Am Your Sign*
Keep it 100 w/Sean and Christa podcast host

The topic of angels is fascinating, vast, and powerful. Years ago, I can remember Paul Cain saying, "if you talk about them, they will appear." There is so much to learn about the supernatural realm and the function and assignments of angels, fulfilling their purpose to serve the heirs of salvation (Hebrews 1:14). In this book, *Secrets of the Angels*, Jamie Galloway has opened our eyes further to the mysteries of the angelic realm. This book will not only broaden our understanding of the supernatural angelic activity that goes on around us all the time but expand our minds and make us more aware of the angelic help we have been given by God. Having had many angelic encounters myself over the years, I am excited to endorse Jamie's book as we navigate this new heightened spiritual era, where Heaven is manifesting here on earth and angels are more frequently appearing to us. Jamie Galloway is a good friend and trusted leader. I highly recommended *Secrets of the Angels* as a valid resource to open our understanding and ignite our spiritual hunger.

—Cindy McGill
Author of *What Your Dreams are Telling You* and *Words that Work*
www.cindymcgill.org

I have been around Jamie's ministry for over a decade. The fruit of his ministry and his constant pursuit of God is astounding. When he shares a story of an encounter, I listen. *Secrets of the Angels* shares clear teaching from Scripture as well as current examples of angelic activity from his own life. It will increase your faith and hunger for more spiritual activity in your own life.

—John E. Thomas
President, Streams Ministries International

I have had the joy and privilege to walk through life with Jamie for over 20 years and to witness his personal experiences and testimonies with the supernatural firsthand. Jamie enlightens us all by sharing his walk with the Lord in powerful moments and insights into scriptures. Jamie dives into a topic misunderstood and abused by many and brings a simplicite and demystified experience.

—Will Hart
Iris Global CEO

SECRETS
OF THE
Angels

DESTINY IMAGE BOOKS BY JAMIE GALLOWAY

Secrets of the Seer

SECRETS
OF THE
Angels

KEYS TO WORKING
WITH HEAVEN'S MESSENGERS

JAMIE GALLOWAY

DESTINY IMAGE® PUBLISHERS, INC.
P.O. Box 310, Shippensburg, PA 17257-0310
"Promoting Inspired Lives."

This book and all other Destiny Image and Destiny Image Fiction books are available at Christian bookstores and distributors worldwide.

For more information on foreign distributors, call 717-532-3040.
Reach us on the Internet: www.destinyimage.com.

ISBN 13 TP: 978-0-7684-5966-1
ISBN 13 eBook: 978-0-7684-5967-8
ISBN 13 HC: 978-0-7684-5969-2
ISBN 13 LP: 978-0-7684-5968-5

For Worldwide Distribution, Printed in the U.S.A.
1 2 3 4 5 6 7 8 / 26 25 24 23 22

CONTENTS

FOREWORD

If you are all about King Jesus and His Kingdom, you cannot afford to be ignorant of the ministry of His angels. If you are watchful in these last days, you are going to see more and need to know more about angels because the role of angels will greatly increase as we quickly approach the coming of the Lord.

Evidence that angels will have an increased role during the end times is found in the Gospel of Matthew, *"So it will be at the end of the age. The angels will come forth"* (Matthew 13:49). This increase in angelic activity means we must get serious in our skillful interaction with God's holy messengers. Angels are stepping up, and so should we. This book is going to help you better understand the role of angels.

A SERIOUS AND SOLVABLE PROBLEM

Most of us do not understand angelic activity. Within the angelic realm are secrets that should not be secrets to God's sons and daughters. Some of these secrets are just now being revealed for the great end-time harvest. This emerging revelation requires interaction and cooperation on our part as believers. How do we know what God has already revealed in this supernatural territory?

There is a lot of false and dangerous information about angels from New Age Gnostics, mystics, witches, and weirdos. You have to sift through so much junk to find the truth, and this can be exhausting. There is a call for true biblical understanding and prophetic Kingdom insight of angels and their various roles.

This book was written to share proper insight into angelic activity and combat false teachings on angels.

AN INTRODUCTION

I am a friend of Jamie Galloway's, and this book reminds me of the many conversations we have had through the years. His content is edgy and interesting. It might challenge you, but you can trust this guy to be all about the Lord Jesus Christ and His Kingdom coming. To demonstrate Jamie's passion for the Kingdom of God, I believe it would be fitting for me to include my introduction to Jamie in this introduction to his book.

It was the summer of 2016. I was turning fifty years old, and during this season of my life, everything was changing. I was going to a whole new level in ministry. John Paul Jackson's team, Steve and Jenny Maddox, had just filmed several episodes with me for *Dreams and Mysteries*. I was in a brand-new world of media ministry and felt like I was way in over my head.

I was on stage at OpenDoor Church, wrapping up another session, when I heard the Spirit of the Lord say, "Here comes your new best friend."

I thought, *That was an odd thing to think*. Just then, the door opened, and Jamie walked down the long aisle toward the stage. From far off, I thought he might be a kid, maybe even a teenager, but as he approached, I saw he was in his mid-thirties. Smiling and confident as always, he came right up to the edge of the stage. I had no idea who he was, what he did, or why he was even there. I just knew we were supposed to become friends, so I went down to meet him.

Since that day, we have traveled, preached, and done life together. I had the honor of officiating his wedding as he married Suzan. My wife, Leanna, and I love Suzan, and Leanna and Suzan do ministry together. In all the thousands of hours of ministry and conversation we have had among the four of us, I can tell you Jamie is always talking about angels. Jamie is an expert on angels—not just in biblical study about angels, but also in personal experience. In fact, I find it hard to hang around Jamie without having supernatural things happen to me, and most of these experiences are angelic.

ANGELS ON ASSIGNMENT

"Did you have a dream with an angel in it last night?" This is a typical morning conversation for people who know Jamie. I was still drinking coffee and trying to wake up when I heard what Jamie asked me but wasn't quick to respond. I am not quick to do anything early in the morning. My back porch is a place of serenity, and Jamie was making me think too hard for so early in the morning.

"No, I don't think so," I said.

"That's weird because I think God told me an angel was coming to give you a word from Him."

That same night, I had a dream, and an angel from the Lord gave me a game-changing word of encouragement and instruction that brought me much closer to Jesus.

Angelic experiences come with Jamie's faith and revelation gift. Expect similar experiences to happen to you once you prayerfully engage in this anointed book .

NO OPPORTUNITY WASTED (NOW)

Nothing is wasted in the Kingdom. God uses every opportunity He has to invade our space and reign in our lives. Your time with Jamie and this powerful study of the angelical realm is going to produce the fruit of the Spirit in your life. As you go through Jamie's book, your knock on God's door to the angelic will be answered in a dramatic way. Jesus will be faithful to answer your knock. That's what I am believing for all who read Jamie's book.

These are exciting times of revelation and unprecedented cooperation between God's human family and God's divine family to see His Kingdom come. Let the journey begin.

—Troy Brewer
Senior/Founding Pastor of OpenDoor Church
Burleson, TX
Author of *Redeeming Your Timeline*
TroyBrewer.com

INTRODUCTION

As I write this book, the wonderful fear of the Lord compels me to prepare you for what you are about to read. This book is unlike any other book I have written. I have included many personal moments with God that have marked my understanding of the angelic realm. The stories I have included make me feel vulnerable because of how sacred these moments have been to me. Though my stories are personal and perhaps even subjective, I would propose that the stories we read in Scripture were once personal to those individuals within the stories. However, I am also honest with myself that the stories within Scripture will always outrank any personal experience I've had.

I feel compelled to communicate clearly to you the importance of the authority of Scripture. I hold to a conviction that the Word of God should be the primary basis for all interpretation of supernatural occurrences. For this reason, we will explore the unique stories of angelic ministry found throughout the narrative of Scripture and seek a greater understanding as to what these scriptural accounts can tell us about the unseen realm.

From time to time, you will read portions from books of the pseudepigraphica. These are never inserted to infer equality with Scripture. I consider some of these literary works helpful to understand the context of Second Temple Jewish perceptions of these topics of which writers of the New Testament would have been aware. There have been many modern books that have influenced my thinking on the

Kingdom of Heaven and what Christian life means to me. And though I appreciate and recommend various modern Christian literature, it is never meant to diminish the superiority of Scripture and its authority in a believer's life. The same is true for ancient literature that contains biblical tones. I view those writings as helpful, though I do not receive them with the same authority as the canon of Scripture.

Finally, my intention for writing *Secrets of the Angels* is to communicate the wonder, majesty, and supremacy of the Father, Son, and Holy Spirit. However mighty they seem to appear in Scripture or other instances, angels are inferior to the Godhead. The Kingdom of Heaven is a Kingdom, which means it has a King. That King is Jesus, and He is ruler of all of Heaven's armies. To assume the King would do everything Himself in His Kingdom is untrue. King Jesus has angels that serve Him as messengers and delegates to accomplish Kingdom purpose. I set out to write a book that would help give language to the often misunderstood subject of angels and their role in the Kingdom of God. This book will not contain an exhaustive library of everything regarding angels; however, my hopes are for it to lay a foundation for understanding the unseen realm and to give you some building blocks to work from as you seek those things which are above.

If then you were raised with Christ, seek those things which are above, where Christ is, sitting at the right hand of God. Set your mind on things above, not on things on the earth.

—Colossians 3:1–2

CHAPTER 1

THE SECRET OF THE ANGELS

*To them it was revealed that, not to themselves, but to
us they were ministering the things which now have
been reported to you through those who have preached
the gospel to you by the Holy Spirit sent from
heaven—things which angels desire to look into.*

—1 Peter 1:12

*Every visible thing in this world is put
in the charge of an Angel.*

—Saint Augustine[1]

Something has been following you and watching over you from the day you came into this world. From the moment your heart took its first beat to the time of your first breath, Heaven has assigned a secret messenger to you, and that messenger has been and will continue to be with you throughout your entire life's journey.

Angels are God's secret messengers, sent from His very presence. Some of us may have sensed their nearness at certain times, but for the most part, angels remain anonymous citizens of an unseen world.

Maybe you have had some unexplainable experiences in your life that made you wonder if angelic activity was involved. I have had a few of those myself. Perhaps you had a close call or two that could not have been averted unless Heaven had offered some inconspicuous help. Moments like these are like fingerprints that cannot be seen. They link the presence of an angel or angels to the scene, but just because their fingerprints remain unseen does not mean angels remain unreal. Angels are more real and more active than anything we could imagine.

Throughout my childhood, I had several encounters that were mysteriously supernatural. These experiences have left me wondering, *Was that an angel?* The Scriptures encourage us to anticipate interaction with the angels, informing us, *"Do not forget to entertain strangers, for by so doing some have unwittingly entertained angels"* (Heb. 13:2). The kindness you share with unknown people is not unknown to Heaven, and I am convinced there are times when angels have blended in so well with the world around us that they can pay us a visit while concealing the reality of who they are. One such occasion happened to me.

In Orlando, Florida, while enjoying a time of rest and recharge, a young boy was found lifeless in the bottom of the lazy river at a local resort. About halfway into a beautiful day, the boy's mother began screaming over him, "My only son! My only son!" All those at the pool watched helplessly as this mother desperately cried for the life of her only son.

By the time the boy was being taken into the ambulance, there was no sign of life. I followed the mother out of the pool as she watched her son being loaded into the ambulance. Her face had the look of terror and confusion, and I could not stand by any longer. In the distress of the

22

moment, I walked up to the mother, took her hands, and asked her for the boy's name. "Adam," she said with tears streaming down her face.

"We are going to pray for Adam," I then told her.

"Please!" she said in her desperation.

As I held the mother's hands, we began to pray. People all around us huddled up against us and started praying. I then said, "Adam, I call your spirit back into your body!"

Voices all around us were shouting prayers for this mother and her only son.

Within a moment, the EMT jumped out of the ambulance and shouted, "The boy is awake! He is okay!"

The mother stood there in shock, yelling, "Praise Jesus! Thank You, Jesus!"

Everyone was asked to leave the pool, so I picked up my son, and we began the journey back to our parked car. As I was loading my son into his seat, I noticed a man standing in front of a vehicle parked directly in front of mine. He stood there staring at me with a smile on his face. As I walked around the side of the car to the driver's side door, I looked at the man, nodded my head, and sort of half smiled to acknowledge him. He looked at me and said, "Hi, Jamie."

"Hi," I responded, a bit stunned and intrigued about how he knew my name.

"Is the boy okay?" the man asked me.

"Yes."

With a confident smile on his face, he looked at me and said, "Good." He then got in his vehicle and I in mine.

I did not immediately drive away. I could not. The only thing I could think of was, *How did he know my name?* Between the boy coming back to life and this strange man knowing my name, I was going to need a while to process all that had just taken place.

There are more details about this moment written in my book *Secrets of the Seer*. But what was not recorded in that book was something interesting that happened over a year later.

I did not always have a strong walk with God; in fact, at a certain time in my youth, I had no walk with God. It was not strong or even weak; it was nonexistent. So, when I did finally turn my life over to Jesus, it felt as if I had just made the biggest discovery in all of human history. My entire life took a dramatic turn, and God seemed to be constantly sending me messages as if we were playing catch up for the years lost.

One night, I woke up to something unusual. I was half asleep and half awake. My body was still sleeping, yet my mind was alert. The scientific community has different names for this type of phenomena, but the Scriptures call it a "trance" (see Acts 10:10). As my body lay there, my mind was alerted to a sound I could hear in my room. I could not see what was happening; my eyes were still shut, and I could not open them. However, my ears heard something I will never forget. It was the sound of angels talking to one another. It all happened so fast, and I was so overwhelmed I could not really take in what they were talking about. The only thing I heard was one angel calling out to another angel by his name.

You are probably thinking, *What is his name?!* Well, it is not important for me to share the name of the angel as it might distract from the important point of this story. What is important for us to know is that, just as God *"counts the number of the stars; He calls them all by name,"* He also knows the number of the angels and gives them each a name (Ps. 147:4). There are very few references to the names of the angels in Scripture. Michael and Gabriel are the only angels in the entire Scripture mentioned by name (see Dan. 8:15–16; 9:21; 10:13, 21; 12:1; Luke 1:19, 26; Jude 1:9; Rev. 12:7). Other angels remain anonymous, but their help is nonetheless as important when they appear.

You may be asking, "Where did the angel go? Did it ever return?" Well, almost seventeen years after that encounter, something unexpected took place. I was sound asleep after returning from a long trip overseas. The international flight arrived very late, and I was so exhausted that I fell asleep in the same clothes I arrived home in.

In the middle of the night, I was instantly awakened to the sound of something walking in front me. Whatever it was, it felt holy, and I could sense the tangible manifestation of God's presence. I could not move the rest of my body, but my eyes were wide open and following the movements of this visitor walking in front of me. I did not even have to ask its name. I was made aware it was the same angel who was called out by name in the middle of the night over seventeen years before, and there he was standing in front of me!

The angel had a message that he spoke out loud, as if he were speaking a declaration over a stadium audience. His message was, "God is going to anoint His Josephs. He will take them out of the dungeon. He will teach them to take one and make it two. He will teach them to take two and make it four." The very second that he ended his proclamation, he vanished. I could still sense him there, but I could not see him. I lay there stunned again by the message of this angel and equally stunned it was the same angel present in my room over seventeen years before. The message he left with me has now been an ongoing revelation to me about the purpose of God I have been carrying for the last several years.

About a year after the miracle in Orlando, I had been traveling around the world speaking on the unseen realm of the angelic and the Kingdom of God. At times, I would share the story of the mysterious man standing in front of my parked car, the man who greeted me by my name. Over and over and over that day, I had tried to make sense of how that man knew my name. Nothing had made sense. The only conclusion I could come to since that day was the man must have been an angel.

During that time, I was speaking at a church in Michigan. I shared the story of the life-giving miracle boy and the man who knew me by name when the awe of God's presence came into the room where we all were gathered. The meeting closed, and everyone was dismissed to lunch break. I went back into the pastor's office, still under the weight of the awe of God. One of the pastors on staff asked me if someone could share with me a vision she had during the last session. I was told this person was a known "seer" in the community. She had a solid track record of prophetic words that had recognizably come to pass. They brought her into the back and introduced us. What she was about to tell me would forever solidify my understanding of the role of angels in our lives.

She began by telling me that, as I had shared about the man who knew my name, the Spirit of God opened her eyes to see in the unseen realm. While I may seem like the first person to be open to hear just about any vision or dream, to be fair, I am not. I learned something early in the prophetic: Not all visions are from the Spirit of God. Just as every prophetic word needs to be judged, the same goes for every vision (see 1 Cor. 14:29). I was taking what she was saying in as she continued to share the vision. In her vision, she saw my vehicle, the same vehicle parked in the parking lot, now moving with angels spread out on both sides of the vehicle. Each of them was moving together in unity, propelling my car forward. And at the front of the car was the man. He was no longer in plain clothes but was revealed to her as an angel sent from the presence of God. She described the angel and his mannerisms. And then she shared his name.

My jaw dropped. I could not believe what I was hearing. I was in a state of shock. My entire being flooded with the presence of glory as she shared his name. It was the name of the angel I heard almost two decades earlier; the same angel who walked before me speaking about

God's Josephs who are coming out of the dungeon with an anointing for increase. And this amazing seer had seen the angel's involvement in the miraculous administration of God's miracle for that precious child.

You see, angels are involved in far more than we realize. And angels are assigned to you and me to accomplish the purposes of God and assist Him with His sovereign administration of the Kingdom of Heaven on Earth.

TOUCHED BY AN ANGEL

The community of believers in the early church were not ignorant of the involvement of angels in the affairs of humanity. During a time of great persecution, the early church faced tremendous adversity that constantly required divine intervention. The apostle Peter had been held as a prisoner by Herod, the king of Judea. His intention was to bring Peter, a public enemy because of his profound message of Jesus' gospel, to public trial after Passover in order to please the people of Judea. Peter was being held in prison until Passover had ended. While kept in chains, prisoner Peter was about to receive a visitor from the outside.

> *Now behold, an angel of the Lord stood by him, and a light shone in the prison; and he struck Peter on the side and raised him up, saying, "Arise quickly!" And his chains fell off his hands. Then the angel said to him, "Gird yourself and tie on your sandals"; and so he did. And he said to him, "Put on your garment and follow me." So he went out and followed him, and did not know that what was done by the angel was real, but thought he was seeing a vision.*
>
> —Acts 12:7–9

Peter did not realize that what he had seen was real. He thought it was a vision. I like to call this the angel of jailbreak! When the jailbreak angel had led Peter all the way out, Peter said to himself, *"Now I know for certain that the Lord has sent His angel, and has delivered me from the hand of Herod and from all the expectation of the Jewish people"* (Acts 12:11). Peter had been touched by an angel.

Later, when he arrived at the house of intercessors who had been praying for his release, those who were gathered could not believe it was actually Peter! The young girl who heard the knock at the door ran in to tell everyone that Peter was standing outside; however, they failed to take her seriously. *"But they said to her, 'You are beside yourself!' Yet she kept insisting that it was so. So they said, 'It is his angel'"* (Acts 12:15). One of the most eye-opening statements about how the early church viewed the role of angels among them is, *"It is his angel."* Remember, these are not naïve young believers. They have served alongside the apostles and now were hosting a prayer gathering at their house to pray through Passover.

It was believed among rabbis that angels may take on the form and likeness of the person to whom they were assigned.[2] Characteristically, as part of their assignment, guardian angels were considered to be the celestial doppelgänger of the one they were entrusted to watch over.[3] When they said, *"It is his angel"* it would have been interpreted through the lens of certain Hebraic literature as Peter's guardian angel (Acts 12:15). Yes, you have a guardian angel! It is an angel that has been assigned to you to watch over you in your journey.

For He shall give His angels charge over you, to keep you in all your ways. In their hands they shall bear you up, lest you dash your foot against a stone.

—Psalm 91:11–12

29

Angels have been assigned to watch and protect you from the time you were born until the time you will be received into Glory. God has commissioned angels to watch over you and fight for you in the unseen realm! Angels stand in the presence of God, waiting for God's voice to instruct them to act on your behalf. Jesus said it like this, *"Take heed that you do not despise one of these little ones, for I say to you that in heaven their angels always see the face of My Father who is in heaven"* (Matt. 18:10). God is sending angels to stand guard over you and battle the forces of darkness that have been against you!

After the jailbreak angel set Peter free, it seems the same angel paid a special visit to Herod who had been persecuting followers of Jesus. Herod had become obsessed with his own glory, and the people he ruled over began to worship him. As King Herod sat on his throne, he gave a speech that incited the crowd to worship him, saying, *"The voice of a god and not of a man!"* (Acts 12:22). In that moment, Herod crossed a spiritual boundary with severe consequences. *"Then immediately an angel of the Lord struck him, because he did not give glory to God. And he was eaten by worms and died"* (v. 23). Touched by an angel may sound sweet, but it has different effects for different folks! While Peter was touched by an angel and set free, Herod was touched by an angel and died. The early church was set free from the tyrannical leadership of Herod, and *"the word of God grew and multiplied"* (v. 24).

God is fighting for you! He has sent angels to stand guard and watch over you. Get ready, God is about to send angels your way to give you great victory over the enemy. Angels fight for you!

ANGELS FIGHT FOR YOU

I was on my way to an event where friends of mine from all over were gathering in Texas for a week to seek God's presence for the beginning of the new year. It was 2020, a decade that began with incredible expectations, and we were waiting for Heaven to speak to us about what to prepare for. As I postured my heart to hear what God would say, I saw something. In a split second, a vision flashed through me. I saw a battle taking place in the Spirit, and my dear friend and pastor, Troy Brewer, was being attacked by a principality. The vision unfolded, and I saw the dark angel touch Troy on his side around his rib cage as if the dark angel were inflicting some sort of wound by his touch. I watched, stunned by what I was seeing. Suddenly, a bright angel burst through the vision with a sword and struck down the wicked spirit, while shouting, "Enough!"

Later that night, I found Troy, and when the time was right, I told him what I had seen in the vision. As I informed Troy, I had no other impression but to tell him the enemy was trying to get at him, but God had sent His angels on assignment to destroy the work of the enemy. Troy sat there, and I could imagine the wheels in his head spinning as he sought to understand the meaning of what I had just told him.

The next morning, I woke up ready to go to the event. I made my way to the back room to grab a coffee when Troy pulled me aside. "Jamie, this is crazy." Lifting up his shirt, I could see marks all over his body as if he had just been clawed by a bear. There were no open wounds, but the bruises across his ribs and his side looked like fresh bruises that were turning blue under the skin.

"Troy, what is this?!" I asked completely stunned.

Troy shot back, "It's your vision, bro!" Troy continued to share with me that through the night it was as if he were wrestling something terrible in his dream. The vision was real. He asked me again for details on what I saw. The heavenly angel in the vision came like a burst of bright light with a sword to stop the attack of the afflicting spirit. An invisible enemy was being confronted by a warrior of God's heavenly army, and that moment was more prophetic than we realized at the time.

We are in an invisible war. Angels and demons are fighting in the battle for nations, and we are getting to witness a spiritual conflict that has been waged since the dawn of time. Some of us have eyes to see the battle that is raging. Others are caught in a web of conspiracy theories trying to make sense of what is happening in the world around us. Still others deny what's apparent and seek to get along with madness by playing dumb. And yet, God is moving His angels into position for the greatest showdown in cosmic history.

TROUBLE IN PARADISE

Where does this invisible battle originate? The earliest point of conflict we see between humankind and the forces of darkness was set in the garden of Eden. It is not obvious in the very beginning of the text, but reading further on we find the garden was not only lush with life and vegetation, but it was also a meeting place between the seen and the unseen.

The garden was the epicenter of life on Earth, and it was also the convergence point between the invisible world of angels and the realm of humanity. In the garden, we see the mystical serpent crafting a manipulative strategy to sabotage the paradise between God and man. There are some glaringly obvious components to this story that are not spelled out in words, but the narrative ensures we can walk away with this understanding.

The atmosphere of Eden was overflowing with supernatural activity: Angels sang while God created, God walked in the garden in the cool of the day, and angelic cherubim stood guard over the tree of life (see Gen 3:8, 24; Job 38:7). Life in the garden was a lot more than an ancient zoo. Eden was the supernatural convergence point between the seen and the unseen. Adam and Eve would not have been ignorant to this reality, and at the center of Paradise was uninhibited access to God's presence. Adam and Eve were so familiar with God's presence that they were found hiding in the trees after they sinned because they heard God walking among them in the garden (see Gen. 3:8). This unrestricted access to God allowed them to enjoy unbroken fellowship with the God who lives in the heavenly realm.

Adam and Eve would not have seen the world like you and I do now. It is not hard to fathom that they may have seen heavenly beings in a world like that. The first humans were pure, undefiled, and completely clothed with God's glory. They were given unlimited access to God's presence and were able to see into the realm of God's presence. The invisible world would have been something they experienced as a byproduct of being with God in His glory.

And remember, it was man who was put in charge of naming the animals. The Creator brought every living beast of the field and bird of the air *"to Adam to see what he would call them"* (Gen. 2:19). God used Adam's sight to "see" the identity of the animal. It would not be hard to conclude that Adam was also able to see the invisible nature of the animals. When the serpent in the garden made itself known, Adam and Eve would have seen something about the serpent that intrigued them enough to hold an intelligent conversation with the creature. There had to be more at play here than a rogue reptile, and we see this confirmed in the Scripture as we are introduced to the creature with these words, *"Now the serpent was more cunning than any beast of the field which the Lord God had made"* (Gen. 3:1).

The serpent in the story, therefore, should not be considered a simple snake. The Hebrew word *nāḥāš* is used for this serpent and has several interesting features. The word can be used as a noun like "a serpent," but it can also be used as a verb as well as an adjective. The verb means "diviner," while the use of this word as an adjective can mean "the shining one." The reader would have found the words of Genesis to be an interesting wordplay expressing multiple layers in the identity of the serpent. Put those together, and you start to see the serpent of divination is the shining one.

The reader should already be aware that this serpent was not like any other animal going about its daily business and oddly striking up a conversation with Eve. Notice how the serpent began a conversation with Eve, *"Has God indeed said, 'You shall not eat of every tree of the garden'?"* (Gen. 3:1). Eve's response was entirely unreasonable if you think she was simply talking to a snake. She didn't yell out to Adam, "Hey, Adam, we got a talker here. Check out this snake. He is talking to me in complete sentences!" No. Eve carried on a conversation as if she was reasoning with an intelligent being.

> *And the woman said to the serpent, "We may eat the fruit of the trees of the garden; but of the fruit of the tree which is in the midst of the garden, God has said, 'You shall not eat it, nor shall you touch it, lest you die.'"*
>
> —Genesis 3:2–3

Second, the being called the serpent here was not a surprise appearance to Adam or Eve. Otherwise, upon seeing the serpent, Adam or Eve would have immediately seemed alarmed as if they were seeing something they had never seen before. The obvious lack of shock over the appearance of the serpent should not be overlooked. This was a mystical being that must have been seen regularly in the garden as if his presence was a normal part of everyday life like the presence of every other created thing inhabiting Eden. In Revelation 12:9, we find the serpent was something more than a simple garden snake: *"So the great dragon was cast out, that serpent of old, called the devil and satan, who deceives the whole world; he was cast to the earth, and his angels were cast out with him."* This divine being we know as the enemy was labeled with four descriptive identities.

1. the great dragon

2. the serpent of old

3. the devil

4. satan

The enemy's identity as the "serpent of old" was the first supernatural being outside of the Creator that we see in the garden narrative. When we recognize this, we begin to see how the garden was not just a paradise on Earth; it was the convergence point between Heaven and Earth. The garden was the spiritual epicenter of the physical and nonphysical world. There were elements in Genesis at play that were not made clear until later in the Scripture, where God recounted the untold moments of our genesis. For example, in Job 38:4, God said, *"Where were you when I laid the foundations of the earth? Tell Me, if you have understanding."* Surely this incredible feat was accomplished with an audience present for such a cosmic event. The Lord continued,

> *Who determined its measurements? Surely you know! Or who stretched the line upon it? To what were its foundations fastened? Or who laid its cornerstone, when the morning stars sang together, and all the sons of God shouted for joy?*
>
> —Job 38:5–7

Whenever God made an appearance throughout Scripture, angelic beings often accompanied him. God is identified as *"the Lord of hosts, who dwells between the cherubim"* (1 Sam. 4:4). In Isaiah's vision, we see the Lord surrounded by Seraphim. It reads, *"Each one had six wings: with two he covered his face, with two he covered his feet, and with two he flew"* (Isa. 6:2). My point is that, where God is, angelic beings are seen accompanying Him. The garden would have experienced a similar dynamic.

Adam and Eve would have seen into a realm of the angelic on a level that prophets and those after them only had a rare opportunity. Angels would have been part of the ambiance of the garden. For all Adam and Eve knew, this would have been normal. Eden was the celestial dwelling place of God on Earth, a type of the heavenly reality pictured as the abode of God. So, for them to see a *shining one* like a *serpent*, or any other supernatural beings, would have been a bit more common inside the garden.

With that in mind, you can see that this was no snake, and you can understand then how difficult it is to see how Adam and Eve, made in the genius of God with enough advanced intelligence to rule the planet, would have been tricked by a mere reptile.

THE TREE OF KNOWLEDGE

Adam and Eve would have seen divine beings more often than we realize. In the prophetic visions given to Enoch, we read about the tree of the knowledge of good and evil (see Gen. 2:9, 17). Enoch, the seventh from Adam, has very little written of him in the cannon of Scripture. We read about Enoch and his unusual walk with God,

> *After he begot Methuselah, Enoch walked with God three hundred years, and had sons and daughters. So all the days of Enoch were three hundred and sixty-five years. And Enoch walked with God; and he was not, for God took him.*
>
> —Genesis 5:22–24

And that's about all we get in the Old Testament regarding Enoch. What did Enoch see in his walk with God? The book of First Enoch documents the visions given to Enoch. While I do not believe the book of Enoch merits canonical authority, I do believe it is an important document containing messages respected by those of Jesus' day as important first-century religious literature. First Enoch tells us of a vision Enoch described as the paradise of righteousness.

> 3 I passed by the paradise of righteousness, and I saw from afar trees more plentiful and larger than these trees, differing from those—very large <and> beautiful and glorious and magnificent—and the tree of wisdom, whose fruit the holy ones eat and learn great wisdom. 4 That tree is in height like the fir, and its leaves, like (those of) the carob, and its fruit like the clusters of the vine—very cheerful; and its fragrance penetrates far beyond the tree. 5 Then I said, "How beautiful is the tree and how pleasing in appearance." 6 Then <Gabriel>, the holy angel who was with me, answered, "This is the tree of wisdom from which your father of old and your mother of old, who were before you, ate and learned wisdom. And their eyes were opened, and they knew that they were naked, and they were driven from the garden."

> —1 Enoch 32:3–6[4]

In Enoch's vision, the tree of the knowledge of good and evil from the Genesis account was called the tree of wisdom, "whose fruit the holy ones eat and learn great wisdom" (1 Enoch 32:3). Adam and Eve may have been witnessing this dynamic on a regular basis. While they were enjoying the fruit of every other tree in the garden, they took their eyes off their own plate and started looking at the plate of the holy ones (angels), seeing that the tree empowered these angelic beings with something more than natural energy. The tree of knowledge of good and evil may have supplied the divine beings with a type of wisdom needed for their function.

Adam and Eve began to desire the fruit,

> *So when the woman saw that the tree was good for food,*
> *that it was pleasant to the eyes, and a tree desirable to make*
> *one wise, she took of its fruit and ate. She also gave to her*
> *husband with her, and he ate.*
>
> —Genesis 3:6

The serpent used the lure of the tree to gain wisdom and *"be like God"* (Gen. 3:5). The enemy was not entirely lying as God later spoke to her, *"Behold, the man has become like one of Us, to know good and evil"* (Gen. 3:22).

If you can imagine, the garden was not only man's home, but it also represented the temple of God on Earth. And this temple garden had angelic-like beings coming in and out for the wisdom supplied by the tree of the knowledge of good and evil.

Some may say, "Well, why do they need to eat fruit for wisdom? Doesn't God give wisdom? Can He not simply impart the wisdom to them without the need for eating a fruit?" Why, yes, but the biblical dynamic is much more natural than that. Eat the fruit from the tree of the knowledge of good and evil and become wise knowing what is good and what is bad. However, eat the fruit from the tree of life, and you live forever. Either way, God set it up that, whether wisdom or life, both were supplied through eating each distinct tree's fruit.

If we fail to see the supernaturalness of the garden, we then think humankind has been in a war with the animal kingdom and enemy number one has been a simple garden snake. However, when we look at the garden narrative from a supernatural worldview, we see a battle between humankind and satan. We see the trickery of the rebellious class of angelic beings, of which satan is chief.

Without a doubt, we can say we are in a spiritual battle, but our spiritual warfare conversation has been limited to the subject of negative thoughts as if our battle was only with negative thinking. We are part of a much bigger battle than just "stinking thinking." Surely, that is one aspect of the warfare, but the truth is humans have been at war with rebellious angelic forces from the beginning, yet we are not alone in this fight. We have Heaven's angels fighting on behalf of those whose hearts are aligned to God's image. Paul wrote, *"For we do not wrestle against flesh and blood, but against principalities, against powers, against the rulers of the darkness of this age, against spiritual hosts of wickedness in the heavenly places"* (Eph. 6:12). The dynamics of this warfare were determined by God in the garden when He prophesied the fate of the serpent who is the devil.

> *So the Lord God said to the serpent: "Because you have done this, you are cursed more than all cattle, and more than every beast of the field; on your belly you shall go, and you shall eat dust all the days of your life. And I will put enmity between you and the woman, and between your seed and her Seed; He shall bruise your head, and you shall bruise His heel."*
>
> —Genesis 3:14–15

FOLLOW THE SEED

Maybe you have heard the phrase, "Follow the money." Well, the narrative of Scripture wants us to follow the Seed. The Seed of Eve referred to the conquering spiritual line and spoke of the incredible cosmic battle between the forces of light and the forces of darkness, culminating in the Messiah's birth, death, resurrection, ascension, and victorious return. The seed of the serpent referred to the spiritual DNA manifesting the forces of darkness in opposition to the Kingdom of Heaven. Jesus is the victorious King who was promised to Eve as the Champion bloodline that would crush the head of the serpent. As you read throughout the Bible, you will see the seed of the serpent continually crushed by the Kingdom of God and the seed of the Messiah. The seed of the serpent will morph and take different forms along the way, but God has determined the victory will go to the *"Seed," "Now to Abraham and his Seed were the promises made. He does not say, 'And to seeds,' as of many, but as of one, 'And to your Seed,' who is Christ"* (Gal. 3:16).

Jesus is the Seed. He is the God-man, the incarnate of God. Our terrestrial mindsets would try to partition this revelation, but He is not half human as if the other half is the God part. No! Perhaps this is why He is called *"the One"* (Joel 2:11; Eph. 4:10). Yet, this is also why the Jewish religious sect called the Pharisees could not receive Jesus as the Son of God, saying, *"For a good work we do not stone You, but for blasphemy, and because You, being a Man, make Yourself God"* (John 10:33). They knew the Torah's words, *"Hear, O Israel: The Lord our God, the Lord is one!"* (Deut. 6:4). Explaining this mystery to them would be like trying to articulate what 3D is like to a two-dimensional person. Jesus is the God-man, the Seed promised to Eve. He is fully man and fully God. And you are one with the One! Remember Jesus' prayer to the Father.

> *I do not pray for these alone, but also for those who will*
> *believe in Me through their word; that they all may be one,*
> *as You, Father, are in Me, and I in You; that they also may*
> *be one in Us, that the world may believe that You sent Me.*
> *And the glory which You gave Me I have given them, that*
> *they may be one just as We are one: I in them, and You in Me;*
> *that they may be made perfect in one, and that the world may*
> *know that You have sent Me, and have loved them as*
> *You have loved Me.*
>
> —John 17:20–23

Those who are of the Seed will be a part of the crushing of the serpent's head. Paul the apostle of Messiah, encouraged those who are part of this incredible honor by writing, *"And the God of peace will crush Satan under your feet shortly"* (Rom. 16:20). Unfortunately, many believers continue to wrestle with their own flesh issues instead of accepting the call to wrestle with principalities and powers. Perhaps this explains why it is written, *"Whoever has been born of God does not sin, for His seed remains in him; and he cannot sin, because he has been born of God"* (1 John 3:9). The preoccupation with sin has got to go. We are called to be overcomers, the finest champions that this hour requires, not struggling soldiers. The *secret of the angels* is a key letting you know you are not alone in this fight. Angels are fighting alongside you on your behalf. The vision for my friend Troy is a just a small window into what is happening in the angelic realm. Let's look at the *secret of angels* at work with angelic hosts fighting alongside the saints for total victory.

ANGELS & SAINTS

Revelation 12 outlines a time when we will see the finest champions stand up with the help of angels in a great end-time battle.

*And war broke out in heaven: Michael and his angels fought
with the dragon; and the dragon and his angels fought,
but they did not prevail, nor was a place found for them in
heaven any longer. So the great dragon was cast out, that
serpent of old, called the devil and satan, who deceives the
whole world; he was cast to the earth, and his angels were
cast out with him.*

—Revelation 12:7–9

One day, the saints will engage in a cosmic battle fought by angels like Michael and those with him against the dragon and his angels. Those in Christ will overcome the great dragon and join with the heavenly hosts to overcome the powers of darkness.

*Then I heard a loud voice saying in heaven, "Now salvation,
and strength, and the kingdom of our God, and the power of
His Christ have come, for the accuser of our brethren, who
accused them before our God day and night, has been cast
down. And they overcame him by the blood of the Lamb and
by the word of their testimony, and they did not love their lives
to the death."*

—Revelation 12:10–11

The angelic armies of Heaven will engage in a battle to rid the heavens of every demonic principality. At that time, the saints of the Kingdom will overcome the enemy by the blood of the Lamb and the word of their testimony. There are angelic forces fighting on the side of the Kingdom of Light, and there are spiritual hosts of wickedness warring against the saints. In *Secrets of the Seer*, ten keys were offered to help you begin your seeing journey. As you dive into this book, my hope is your understanding will transform from a terrestrial worldview to that of a celestial worldview and give you keys to partner with Heaven's messengers. This is *Secrets of the Angels*.

As we take this journey into the mysteries of the angelic realm, pray this prayer with me:

Father, I come to You with childlike faith believing Your Word to be made manifest in my life. I am looking with expectation for the realm of Your presence to open my eyes. Even as angels surround You in glory, may the glory of Your goodness surround me. Your Word declares, "The angel of the Lord encamps all around those who fear Him, and delivers them" (Ps. 34:7). Let the promise of Your Word become a living testimony in me. In Jesus' name, amen.

NOTES

1. Saint Augustine, *Eighty-Three Different Questions (The Fathers of the Church, Volume 70): A New Translation*, trans. David L. Mosher (Washington, DC: Catholic University of America Press, 1982), 200. www.jstor.org/stable/j.ctt32b1xb.

2. Dr. Michael S. Heiser with Residential Layman Trey Stricklin, The Naked Bible Podcast 2.0, podcast transcription, May 10, 2015, https://www.nakedbiblepodcast.com/wp-content/uploads/2015/05/Transcript-48-Acts-1112.pdf.

3. Andrei A. Orlov (Marquette University), *The Heavenly Counterpart Traditions in the Pseudepigrapha about Jacob*, "Jacob's Heavenly CounterpartinRabbinicAccounts"https://www.marquette.edu/maqom/jacob88.html#sdfootnote39anc.

4. George W. E. Nickelsburg and James C. VanderKam, *1 Enoch: The Hermeneia Translation* (Minneapolis: Fortress Press, 2012), 47–48, Kindle.

CHAPTER 2

THE SECRET OF
THE WATCHERS

*"I saw in the visions of my head while on my bed, and there
was a watcher, a holy one, coming down from heaven."*

—Daniel 4:13

*Yes, the entrance of sin into God's good world occurred in Eden,
but the unanimous testimony of Second Temple Judaism is that the
Watchers are to blame for the proliferation of evil on the earth.*

—Dr. Michael S. Heiser[1]

What began in the garden did not stop there. The accounts of this supernatural dynamic are strung throughout the narrative of Scripture. Angelic forces are warring against each other in the unseen realm, and the ruling powers of darkness have shown their cards. They want to keep you out of your land of promise. They want to possess your land and run you off from the face of the earth. It started in the garden, and only ten generations from Adam, we see the supernatural enemies of God's plan at work again, crafting a plan to thwart God's cosmic purpose with humanity. This is the *secret of the watchers.*

THE ANTEDILUVIAN AGE

Between the fall of man in the garden and the flood of Noah on the earth, the period of time between those two events is known as the antediluvian period. The antediluvian age was a time of supernatural extremes. Imagine the sexual revolution of the 1960s on steroids, only this was not isolated to a farm in upstate New York; this was the whole of humanity. The earth was still so young; humanity was fallen yet still so innocent. Because of the innocence, it was a time where the separating veil between the seen and unseen realms was nearly non-existent. Spiritual realities coexisted alongside the natural world in such a heightened way that angels and humans were mixing with one another.

Much mystery remains around the stories of that period, but there are some things mentioned in Genesis that give us clues to piece together a picture of what may have happened. The days leading up to the great flood were a time of unprecedented supernatural activity, unlocking an information age that nearly ruined humankind forever, but God had a plan.

Angelic beings known as the elohim, members of the invisible race, had made themselves visible to humanity, teaching them the art of deceit, war making, witchcraft, and death. The letter of Jude comments on these beings, stating, *"And the angels who did not keep their proper domain, but left their own abode, He has reserved in everlasting chains under darkness for the judgment of the great day"* (Jude 1:6). The angelic forces left the heavenly realm and paid a visit to humanity.

*Now it came to pass, when men began to multiply on the face
of the earth, and daughters were born to them, that the sons of
God saw the daughters of men, that they were beautiful; and
they took wives for themselves of all whom they chose.*

—Genesis 6:1–2

The term *"sons of God"* is used to describe the members of God's
divine council. The Hebrew word found in Genesis 6:1–2 being
translated *sons of God* is *bēn* (the sons) *'ĕlōhîm* (of God). Scholars
believe that the ruling class of angelic beings who governed together
with God in the unseen realm were members of a divine council.[2] This
divine council consisted of the sons of God, but as the story unfolds
around the members of the divine council, we begin to see a narrative
of rebellion among the sons of God detailed in Psalm 82:1 and 6:

*1 God ['ĕlōhîm] stands in the congregation of the mighty; He
judges among the gods ['ĕlōhîm].*

*6 I said, "You are gods ['ĕlōhîm], and all of you are children
of the Most High [bēn 'elyôn].*

The easiest way to understand this is to recognize that angels are
not human as you and I are members of the human race. Angels are
members of the unseen realm, created by God to rule with Him in His
divine council. Elohim is not a word restricted to God alone, but it is an
identifying term used to describe nonphysical beings. If you can recall
the story of the witch of Endor, there is an interesting detail found in
her dialogue with King Saul. Saul was looking for a medium who could
conduct a séance for him to bring up someone from the dead (see 1 Sam.
28:7–8). Speaking to the dead is a forbidden ritual according to the law:

When you come into the land which the Lord your God is giving you, you shall not learn to follow the abominations of those nations. There shall not be found among you anyone who makes his son or his daughter pass through the fire, or one who practices witchcraft, or a soothsayer, or one who interprets omens, or a sorcerer, or one who conjures spells, or a medium, or a spiritist, or one who calls up the dead. For all who do these things are an abomination to the Lord, and because of these abominations the Lord your God drives them out from before you.

—Deuteronomy 18:9–12

Saul was king and thought he was above God's law. The hypocrisy of the story is the witch confronted Saul, who had disguised himself, and she said to him, *"Look, you know what Saul has done, how he has cut off mediums and the spiritists from the land. Why then do you lay a snare for my life, to cause me to die?"* (1 Sam. 28:9).

Saul swore to her, *"As the Lord lives, no punishment shall come upon you for this thing"* (v. 10).

Who was Saul seeking from the realm of the dead?

Saul spoke to the witch, *"Bring up Samuel for me"* (v. 11).

Samuel had been deceased for some time, but Saul was desperate for a prophetic fix. God was not speaking to him any longer *"by dreams or by Urim or by the prophets"* (v. 6). Saul was attempting to conjure up his trusted prophet, Samuel, from the afterlife.

When the woman saw Samuel, she cried out with a loud
voice. And the woman spoke to Saul, saying, "Why have you
deceived me? For you are Saul!" And the king said to her,
"Do not be afraid. What did you see?" And the woman said to
Saul, "I saw a spirit ['ĕlōhîm] ascending out of the earth."

1 Samuel 28:12 13

The *'ĕlōhîm* mentioned here was the spirit of Samuel the prophet. Saul ultimately met his doom as we find Saul's prophecy from the dead prophet detailed that Saul would be joining him the following day in the afterlife (v. 19)

THE SIN OF THE WATCHERS

The term *watchers* has come to be recognized as an identification given to the sons of God. The *bēn 'ĕlōhîm* are regarded by many scholars as the watchers spoken about in Daniel when King Nebuchadnezzar dreamed about the decree of the watchers concerning the next seven years.

And inasmuch as the king saw a watcher, a holy one, coming
down from heaven and saying, "Chop down the tree and
destroy it, but leave its stump and roots in the earth, bound
with a band of iron and bronze in the tender grass of the field;
let it be wet with the dew of heaven, and let him graze with the
beasts of the field, till seven times pass over him"; this is the
interpretation, O king, and this is the decree of the Most High,
which has come upon my lord the king: They shall drive you
from men, your dwelling shall be with the beasts of the field,

and they shall make you eat grass like oxen. They shall wet
you with the dew of heaven, and seven times shall pass over
you, till you know that the Most High rules in the kingdom of
men, and gives it to whomever He chooses.

—Daniel 4:23–25

It is essential to the discussion that we understand the *'ĕlōhîm* are a central focus of a supernatural worldview. God's dealings with the watchers and their progeny are riddled throughout the narrative of the Scriptures. While modern preachers place the emphasis of sin upon Adam and Eve, it was the watchers (*'ĕlōhîm*) who furthered man's sin intelligence by teaching mankind all sorts of demonic behavior, instructing them in what Scripture calls *"the depths of Satan"* (Rev. 2:24).

The book of Enoch details the type of knowledge that was being taught to humanity through these rebellious watchers.

You see what Asael has done, who has taught all iniquity on the earth, and has revealed the eternal mysteries that are in heaven, <which the sons of men were striving to learn.>[3]

The watchers took it upon themselves to teach mankind the depths of wickedness not previously known:

• Instruments of war for the making of violence (1 Enoch 8:1).

• The crafting of jewelry and makeup for men and women to wear for the manipulation of seduction (1 Enoch 8:1).

- The art of spell making and psychedelics from the roots of plants (1 Enoch 7:1; 8:3).[4]

- The knowledge of astrology, for the reading of signs and the worship of celestial bodies (1 Enoch 8:3).

- The knowledge of all sins, and how to make hate-inducing charms (1 Enoch 9:8).

- The knowledge of all the blows of death, including how to inflict blows of the fetus in the womb, to cause it to abort (1 Enoch 69:6, 12).

- The knowledge of how to make hate-inducing charms (1 Enoch 9:8).

The list can go on and on, but I think you get the point—these are some nasty characters. As we look into the sin of watchers, something else stands out that is the central focus of the Genesis 6 narration of the watchers.

Now it came to pass, when men began to multiply on the face of the earth, and daughters were born to them, that the sons of God saw the daughters of men, that they were beautiful; and they took wives for themselves of all whom they chose.

—Genesis 6:1–2

There were giants on the earth in those days, and also afterward, when the sons of God came in to the daughters of men and they bore children to them. Those were the mighty men who were of old, men of renown.

—Genesis 6:4

Members of the *'ĕlōhîm (sons of God)* went into the daughters of men and took them as wives. Their union was unnatural, and something demonic came forth from their union, the giants, which we will explore in the next chapter, "The Secrets of the Giants."

IT'S ABOUT NATIONS

The *secret of the watchers* is a key that helps us understand how to partner with Heaven for God's re-inheritance of nations. Under the leadership of the watchers, the nations have rebelled against God's ways. Psalm 82 is considered by scholars as a lament describing their corrupt leadership and God's disapproval of their wickedness, *"God stands in the congregation of the mighty; He judges among the gods. How long will you judge unjustly, and show partiality to the wicked? Selah"* (Ps. 82:1–2).

What will become of these fallen watchers? God declares their doom, "I said, 'You are gods, and all of you are children of the Most High. But you shall die like men, and fall like one of the princes'" (vv. 6–7). The psalm concludes, "Arise, O God, judge the earth; for You shall inherit all nations" (v. 8) The nations have been crying for deliverance from the oppression of principalities, and there is only one who is worthy to inherit the nations, the Man Christ Jesus. How do we partner with Heaven to see Jesus receive the nations as His inheritance?

> *I will declare the decree: The Lord has said to Me, "You are My Son, today I have begotten You. Ask of Me, and I will give You the nations for Your inheritance, and the ends of the earth for Your possession."*
>
> —Psalm 2:7–8

While angels have their positions in the Kingdom, the Scriptures do not give the authority on Earth to angels. There can never be an angel ruling Earth as a king. Angels are made of celestial matter, but God made man from the dust of the earth. In fact, He spoke everything into existence except for man: *"And the Lord God formed man of the dust of the ground, and breathed into his nostrils the breath of life; and man became a living being"* (Gen. 2:7). However, watcher angels are positioned by God to be watchers over the affairs of nations. Michael was mentioned as a watcher appointed with Heaven's authority to watch over the security of the nation of Israel.

> *At that time Michael shall stand up, the great prince who stands watch over the sons of your people; and there shall be a time of trouble, such as never was since there was a nation, even to that time. And at that time your people shall be delivered, every one who is found written in the book.*
>
> —Daniel 12:1

As Michael stands up, a time of trouble begins with the nation of Israel, but the final act of the story will lead to the salvation of all who are written in the book. Watchers like Michael contend with other watchers who are in charge of nations, but who have rebelled from the ways of Yahweh. Daniel described this dynamic when the angel arrived to deliver a message at the end of a twenty-one-day fast:

> *But the prince of the kingdom of Persia withstood me twenty-one days; and behold, Michael, one of the chief princes, came to help me, for I had been left alone there with the kings of Persia.*
>
> —Daniel 10:13

The dynamic of partnership between celestial rulers and kings of the earth was something prophets gave language to. Isaiah's prophetic utterance depicted this mystery, *"It shall come to pass in that day that the Lord will punish on high the host of exalted ones, and on the earth the kings of the earth"* (Isa. 24:21). When the prince of Persia contended with the angelic being sent to deliver to Daniel the word of the Lord, a war broke out, and the watcher of Israel, Michael, came to the aid of the angel who alone was fighting the prince of Persia and the kings of Persia. One controlled the spiritual atmosphere while the others controlled the terrestrial atmosphere.

Unlike the angels who have celestial bodies, God formed man from terrestrial matter, giving us a terrestrial authority to work the ground (see Gen. 2:5; 1 Cor. 15:40). Just as angels will not inherit the earth, angels do not work the ground because that has been given to humankind. You have been given authority to work the ground. As you do, you are shifting things in the heavens and displacing principalities from their seat of influence over regions. Like kings on the earth, you are fighting a war against the kings of nations who are standing in the way of the Kingdom of God. Your actions under the influence of the Spirit of the Living God are backed by Heaven's angelic army for the taking of nations.

So, how did it come to be that the nations came under the leadership of these divine rebels? An often overlooked passage from the Song of Moses contains important insight into the biblical narrative of the *bēn 'ĕlōhîm*. *"When the Most High gave to the nations their inheritance, when he divided mankind, he fixed the borders of the peoples according to the number of the sons of God"* (Deut. 32:8 ESV). While some translations may say, *"according to the number of the children of*

Israel," others like the ESV adhere to the reading of the manuscripts from the Dead Sea Scrolls, which translate this portion of Scripture as *"sons of God."* Moses was making a reference to Genesis 10 and the table of nations. However, Israel was not even born yet, so "sons of Israel" does not seem fitting.

God's plan for the nations was a redemptive plan. God chose to relinquish the governing role over nations to the watchers because God had a plan of redemption that would begin with the seed of Abraham and would be completed in Christ. Through Abraham's seed, God would have *one* nation set apart for Him to bring about the redemption of *all* nations. Follow the seed. God spoke to Abraham, *"In your seed all the nations of the earth shall be blessed, because you have obeyed My voice."* (Gen. 22:18)

I SAW SATAN FALL

If you recall, Genesis 10 divided the earth into seventy unique nations. This is known as the *table of nations*. Fast forward to Jesus sending out *"laborers into His harvest,"* and we read that He appointed seventy of His disciples to go out *"before His face into every city and place where He Himself was about to go"* (Luke 10:1–2). By sending out the seventy, it was as if Jesus was saying, "Go, and get My nations back!"

As the seventy returned, they came bearing good news! They saw for themselves, that the demons were subject to them as they spoke the name of Jesus! This was not surprising at all to Jesus.

Then the seventy returned with joy, saying, "Lord, even the demons are subject to us in Your name." And He said to them, "I saw Satan fall like lightning from heaven."

—Luke 10:17–18

And while they had their eyes on the ground, Jesus had his eyes in the sky. They saw demons flee from the earth while Jesus saw Satan fall like lightning!

At the same time the disciples were taking new territory for the King of Kings, there was a war going on in the realm of angels. Angels of light were fighting against the angels of darkness. The fallen watchers and the kingdom of darkness were being displaced. It was a mirror effect. Whenever we move out in the Kingdom, carrying the name of Jesus to the nations, the satanic watchers are being removed from their seat of authority as we take new ground. Angels are fighting this war with us, and while we take our authority in the earth as sons and daughters of God, the Lord of hosts is going out to war with us, with the angelic forces of Heaven, to displace the ruling spirits over nations. God judges these *"gods"* while we fulfill his command to *"go"* (Ps. 82:6; Matt. 28:19). This corresponding war is demonstrated throughout Scripture.

The kings came and fought, then the kings of Canaan fought in Taanach, by the waters of Megiddo; they took no spoils of silver. They fought from the heavens; the stars from their courses fought against Sisera.

—Judges 5:19–20

The Lord of hosts, the God of Israel, says: "Behold, I will
bring punishment on Amon of No, and Pharaoh and Egypt,
with their gods and their kings—Pharaoh and those who trust
in him."

—Jeremiah 46:25

This mirror effect begins to make more sense for us in the new covenant when Jesus gave the keys of the Kingdom to Peter, saying, *"And I will give you the keys of the kingdom of heaven, and whatever you bind on earth will be bound in heaven, and whatever you loose on earth will be loosed in heaven"* (Matt. 16:19). For this reason, Jesus sends us out into the field of harvest to gather the nations for His inheritance. What we do on Earth matters in the heavens. Jesus said,

Behold, I give you the authority to trample on serpents and
scorpions, and over all the power of the enemy, and nothing
shall by any means hurt you. Nevertheless do not rejoice
in this, that the spirits are subject to you, but rather rejoice
because your names are written in heaven.

—Luke 10:19–20

As we step out to trample on the demonic things that have poisoned the earth (serpents and scorpions), something takes place in the heavenlies. The satanic oppression falls like lightning, and our names are written in their place! Now, the ruling force over a region is no longer a principality of darkness, but the names of God's children are written in that heavenly realm.

KEYS TO ACTIVATING THIS SECRET

"What can I do to partner with Heaven for King Jesus' inheritance of nations? What can I do to work with Heaven's messengers to see the Kingdom come and Jesus' will be done on Earth as it is in Heaven?" These are the questions we must ask ourselves.

Here are some practical steps to walking out the *secret of the watchers* and receiving the nations as your inheritance in Christ.

BE THE LIGHT

Do not hide your brightness any longer! This is your time to shine.

> *You are the light of the world. A city that is set on a hill cannot be hidden. Nor do they light a lamp and put it under a basket, but on a lampstand, and it gives light to all who are in the house. Let your light so shine before men, that they may see your good works and glorify your Father in heaven.*
>
> —Matthew 5:14–16

Remember, "*Those who are wise shall shine like the brightness of the firmament, and those who turn many to righteousness like the stars forever and ever*" (Dan. 12:3).

Stop hiding your bright idea and the gift that God has given you. Angels are waiting for you to step out and reveal the glory of God to those around you!

How can we be the light? Remember God found the *bēn ʿĕlōhîm* of Psalm 82 guilty of judging unjustly and showing favor to the wicked. We are called to take up for their lack of justice and do what they failed to do: *"Defend the poor and fatherless; do justice to the afflicted and needy. Deliver the poor and needy; free them from the hand of the wicked"* (Ps. 82:3–4).

WALK YOUR LAND

The Lord told Abram in Genesis 13:17, *"Arise, walk in the land through its length and its width, for I give it to you."* And Paul told the Roman believers that as children of God we are *"heirs—heirs of God and joint heirs with Christ"* (Rom. 8:17). God made you to be a co-heir with Christ of all things. I encourage you to walk through your city, your county, and your neighborhood, and take note of everything. I believe vision will begin to unfold to you of how you can partner with Heaven to displace the fallen ruling spirits from their place of influence on the land.

Where you see poverty, begin to ask the Holy Spirit to give you keys to unlocking wealth in that place. Where you see hunger and pain, bring food and healing. As you do, you are dismantling the effects of the demonic leadership over that region and making the name of Jesus famous.

ANGELS GO BEFORE YOU

Angels go before you into every place you are about to go. They are preparing the way for you and setting you up for success: *"Behold, I send an Angel before you to keep you in the way and to bring you into the place which I have prepared"* (Exod. 23:20).

Like Ezekiel's vision of the valley of dry bones, God is calling you to a city of dry bones, a nation in need of resurrection life. And as Ezekiel was commanded, make this prophetic declaration over your city of dry bones, *"Thus says the Lord God: 'Come from the four winds, O breath, and breathe on these slain, that they may live'"* (Ezek. 37:9).

Release angels to go before you and bring resurrection life to the broken and the poor. Pray this prayer with me:

Lord of the angel armies, let the forces of Heaven go before me as I carry Your light. Open my eyes to see the hosts of Heaven at work preparing the way for the great end-time harvest of nations. Let angels guard me on every side as I place my feet on the land of Your inheritance!

NOTES

1. Michael S. Heiser, *Reversing Hermon: Enoch, The Watchers, and the Forgotten Mission of Jesus Christ* (Crane, MO: Defender, 2017), 8, Kindle.

2. Michael S. Heiser, *Angels: What the Bible Really Says about God's Heavenly Host* (Bellingham, WA: Lexham Press, 2018), 20.

3. George W. E. Nickelsburg and James C. VanderKam, *1 Enoch: The Hermeneia Translation* (Minneapolis: Fortress Press, 2012), 26, Kindle.

4. "Charlesworth translates: 'And they taught them magical medicine, incantations, the cutting of roots, and taught them (about) plants. The terms in Greek are pharmakeia, epaoida, hrizotomias, and botanas. The first of these (pharmakeia) is found in Revelation 9:21. The term can refer to drugs, poisons, magic potions, and medicines.' These items could have varying levels of potency, from providing mild sedation or a feeling of well-being to being mind-altering." Dr. Michael S. Heiser, *A Companion to the Book of Enoch: A Reader's Commentary, Vol I: The Book of the Watchers* (1 Enoch 1–36) (Crane, MO: Defender, 2020), 133, Kindle.

CHAPTER 3

THE SECRET OF THE GIANTS

There were giants on the earth in those days, and also afterward, when the sons of God came in to the daughters of men and they bore children to them. Those were the mighty men who were of old, men of renown.

—Genesis 6:4

When Columbus first sought this continent—when Christ suffered on the cross—when Moses led Israel through the Red Sea—nay, even when Adam first came from the hand of his Maker—then as now, Niagara was roaring here. The eyes of that species of extinct giants, whose bones fill the mounds of America, have gazed on Niagara, as ours do now.

—Abraham Lincoln[1]

The *secret of the giants* is a powerful key that will identify the spiritual giants currently possessing your land. From the seed of the serpent to the seed of the watchers, the kingdom of darkness has attempted to exile you from the land of your inheritance and continue to keep you out of the land of your promise.

I want to underscore the fact that we are not talking about taller people. Think King Kong on a rampage in New York City endued with supernatural powers. What is more evident is they would not be big and dumb. Due to the angelic DNA in their genetic makeup, the giants had an intelligence advantage over their human counterparts. An evidence of this is their weaponry.

The progeny of the *ĕlōhîm* were absolutely horrific. We are talking worst nightmare level with the supernatural ability to carry advanced armor and weaponry, giving them a gigantic advantage over humanity. Hugh Ross points out his thoughts as an astrophysicist on the supernatural nature of the Nephilim that would defy known laws of physics.

> From a scientific perspective, the stature of Nephilim, Raphaim, and Anakim exceeds human physical capabilities as well as the limits of biological engineering. The bone mass necessary to support muscles and resist gravity's effects rises geometrically with a person's height (just as the weight of a building's supporting beams goes up geometrically with the length of the spans they support). This ratio implies an increasingly severe loss of mobility and stamina once human height exceeds about eight feet.[2]

It is important to understand that these giants were not simply bigger people. Had they operated out of the normal laws of physics like everyone else, they would not have been able to carry the heavy load of armor described in detail in Scripture. Goliath is the main giant that we are familiar with who some estimate to have been between nine feet, nine inches tall to even possibly closer to twelve feet tall.[3] Ross continues his commentary on the giants, noting the giants' capabilities were beyond the laws of physics.

Given human physiological limits, the description of the
Nephilim—if mere men—must be exaggerated. Strictly
natural bodies cannot manifest the stated combination of
size, power, agility, load-carrying capacity, and endurance.
The only other way to maintain this interpretation would be
to question the weights and measures of Moses' and David's
time. This approach presents difficulties, however, in view of
archaeological evidence confirming their consistency, and it
raises the additional problem of why Saul, a soldier who was
"an impressive young man without equal" and "a head taller"
than any other Israelite, was so terrified of Goliath. Likewise,
it raises questions as to why ten of the Israelite spies sent
into the Promised Land by Moses exclaimed, "We saw the
Nephilim there. . . . We seemed like grasshoppers in our own
eyes, and we looked the same to them." Such words could be
taken as hyperbole, but the measurements cannot.[4]

THE SEED OF THE SERPENT

Our main villain from chapter one, the serpent, was cursed by God
confining him to a life of dust licking and belly crawling.

*So the Lord God said to the serpent: "Because you have done
this, You are cursed more than all cattle, and more than every
beast of the field; on your belly you shall go, and you shall eat
dust all the days of your life. And I will put enmity between
you and the woman, and between your seed and her Seed; He
shall bruise your head, and you shall bruise His heel."*

—Genesis 3:14–15

This is not a literal change for the serpent, as if it were a snake with legs previous to the curse. *"On your belly you shall go"* has symbolic connection to the abomination signification attached to any *"creeping thing"* and *"whatever crawls on its belly"* (Lev. 11:41–42). There are clear supernatural realities at work with the war of two seeds. The spiritual implications are evident when God mentions *"her seed."* A woman does not biologically produce a seed, so there must be something else at play in this cosmic drama.

The war between the seed of the serpent and the seed of Eve is the spiritual seed of the line of Eve, leading to Jesus, versus the spiritual seed of the serpent, leading to the antichrist. Those spiritually carrying the seed of each are carefully detailed through the narrative of the Scriptures. As we journey into the rest of this story, I want you to really take in just how much emphasis we are going to find on the seed of the serpent versus the seed of Eve.

The rebellious act of the watchers in Genesis 6 brought about an entirely new race of beings upon the earth that was a literal manifestation of the seed of the serpent: *"There were giants on the earth in those days, and also afterward, when the sons of God came in to the daughters of men and they bore children to them. Those were the mighty men who were of old, men of renown"* (Gen. 6:4). These were mighty men, meaning strong in warfare, and legends were made around their conquests. Think warlords like Genghis Khan or Alexander the Great, only endowed with supernatural size and abilities, and they did not fight for any cause except their own appetites. First Enoch elaborates on their appetites:

> And they conceived from them and bore to them great giants.
> And the giants begot Nephilim, and to the Nephilim were

born †Elioud†. And they were growing in accordance with
their greatness. They were devouring the labor of all the sons
of men, and men were not able to supply them. And the giants
began to kill men and to devour them. And they began to sin
against the birds and beasts and creeping things and the fish,
and to devour one another's flesh. And they drank the blood[5]
(6:2–5).

The giants were an abomination, the offspring of rebellious angels who
had a wicked appetite. They were endowed with otherworldly DNA,
causing their strength to go unmatched. The name given to them by
the writer of Genesis is Nephilim, which consists of the Hebrew root
word *Nephal* and *yim*, meaning fallen ones. The word *Nephilim* means
fallen, attributing them to the progeny of fallen angels. The Nephilim
were infused with the rebellious nature of the fallen watchers and were
operating out of the same defiance toward God's Edenic agenda that
the serpent displayed in the garden. The fallen angels had the same
effect on humanity that the serpent had in the garden, exile from the
land where God's presence dwells.

Goliath's name meant *exile*. Goliath was a literal manifestation of the
spirit that causes exile. What does exile mean? Exile is the enemy's
plan to keep you out of your promised land. It is the seed of the serpent
causing you to be driven out of God's garden. The giants are currently
possessing your promised land, and it is time to recognize this secret
agenda of the enemy and cross over into your promise.

We must realize that our promised land is not void of enemy occupants.
God warned the Israelites of the process by which He planned to
remove the enemies who were occupying Canaan. He commanded the

Israelites, *"Then you shall drive out all the inhabitants of the land from before you, destroy all their engraved stones, destroy all their molded images, and demolish all their high places"* (Num. 33:52). He also warned them, *"But if you do not **drive out the inhabitants of the land** from before you, **then** it shall be that those whom you let remain shall be irritants in your eyes and thorns in your sides, and **they** shall harass you in **the land** where you dwell"* (v. 55).

Fast-forward from Moses to the time of David, and we still see Israel fighting off these giants when David squared off against a formidable foe, Goliath.

Goliath and every other giant were physical manifestations of the seed of the serpent. The *secret of the watchers* gives us a glimpse into the enemy's playbook. You may think that the giants are a thing of the past. And, yes, I do not see any evidence of physical giants returning; however, the spiritual realities of these giants are just as threatening today as ever. If you are going to bring the Kingdom of Heaven to this world, God is asking you to have eyes to see the giants. I see the Lord making a proclamation against the giants that have troubled you.

> *Speak, and say, "Thus says the Lord God: 'Behold, I am against you, O Pharaoh king of Egypt, O great monster who lies in the midst of his rivers, who has said, "My River is my own; I have made it for myself." But I will put hooks in your jaws, and cause the fish of your rivers to stick to your scales; I will bring you up out of the midst of your rivers, and all the fish in your rivers will stick to your scales.'"*
>
> —Ezekiel 29:3–4

IT TAKES A DIFFERENT SPIRIT

Before Israel moved into the Promised Land, Moses, their national leader, picked twelve spies from the tribes of Israel to go into and spy out the land of Canaan. They were sent in with a mission.

Then Moses sent them to spy out the land of Canaan, and said to them, "Go up this way into the South, and go up to the mountains, and see what the land is like: whether the people who dwell in it are strong or weak, few or many; whether the land they dwell in is good or bad; whether the cities they inhabit are like camps or strongholds; whether the land is rich or poor; and whether there are forests there or not. Be of good courage. And bring some of the fruit of the land." Now the time was the season of ripe grapes.

—Numbers 13:17–20

From their deliverance from Egypt to the wars of Moses and the harsh realities of wilderness life, Israel has faced threat after threat. Despite all these challenges, Israel was about to face something they had only heard of in legends.

Then they told him, and said: "We went to the land where you sent us. It truly flows with milk and honey, and this is its fruit. Nevertheless the people who dwell in the land are strong; the cities are fortified and very large; moreover we saw the descendants of Anak there."

—Numbers 13:27–28

The *"descendants of Anak"* were a clan from the giants that possessed the Promised Land. As the twelve spies returned from the Promised Land, the news of the Anakim posed an incredible threat to the tribes of Israel. Attempting to awaken bravery in the weary travelers, one of the twelve named Caleb spoke, *"Let us go up at once and take possession, for we are well able to overcome it"* (v. 30). This was not enough to convince the tribes as the other spies who stood by challenged Caleb's faith with a message of fear:

> *And they gave the children of Israel a bad report of the land*
> *which they had spied out, saying, "The land through which*
> *we have gone as spies is a land that devours its inhabitants,*
> *and all the people whom we saw in it are men of great stature.*
> *There we saw the giants (the descendants of Anak came from*
> *the giants); and we were like grasshoppers in our own sight,*
> *and so we were in their sight."*
>
> —Numbers 13:32–33

This is perhaps one of the most transparent fear statements in all the Scriptures, *"We were like grasshoppers in our own sight, and so we were in their sight."* Their view of themselves became so insignificant, it caused a spiritual reality to form in the enemy's perspective. This is huge. How you perceive yourself will determine your enemy's perception of you! Not every spy had this inferiority mentality. Joshua and Caleb were different.

> *But Joshua the son of Nun and Caleb the son of Jephunneh,*
> *who were among those who had spied out the land, tore their*
> *clothes; and they spoke to all the congregation of the children*

72

THE SECRET OF THE GIANTS

*of Israel, saying: "The land we passed through to spy out is
an exceedingly good land. If the Lord delights in us, then He
will bring us into this land and give it to us, 'a land which
flows with milk and honey.' Only do not rebel against the
Lord, nor fear the people of the land, for they are our bread;
their protection has departed from them, and the Lord is with
us. Do not fear them."*

—Numbers 14:6–9

The *secret of the watchers* revealed the enemy's plan to exile you
from your destiny and keep you from the promised land. The fallen
angels had brought forth giants that began to possess and devour the
land chosen for God's people. You may not realize the enemy's goal is
not just to give you a bad day, but he wants to possess your promised
land. It is vital that you understand the powers, principalities, and
rulers of darkness have brought forth giants to devour and intimidate
you, keeping you out of the promised land. It's time to take back the
land God has called you to. It's time to face the giants that have been
possessing your land.

It is time to stand up like Caleb and Joshua, and proclaim over your
giants, *"They are our bread"* (Num. 14:9). While the giants may be
looking at you, like you're their next meal, you need to look right back
at them, like they are your bread. The only way to face the giants is
with a different spirit. God spoke about Caleb in this way, *"But My
servant Caleb, because he has a different spirit in him and has followed
Me fully, I will bring into the land where he went, and his descendants
shall inherit it"* (Num. 14:24). This sounds to me like God was saying,
"Caleb has a giant man's spirit in a normal man's body." It is time you
start seeing yourself as bigger than the giants you are facing!

The *secret of the watchers* will give you language for the nature of the giants that are devouring your destiny and possessing your land. Let's explore the nature of the Nephilim and see if you can identify which of these have been standing in the way of your promised land.

DRIVE OUT THE GIANTS

The angelic rebellion giving way to the Nephilim created monster beings that very few dared to face. Remember, it was under tall King Saul, who was *"a head taller than anyone else,"* that our most recognized giant, Goliath, is seen terrorizing the armies of Israel (1 Sam. 9:2 NIV). None dared to challenge him, until David. Goliath, the Nephilim manifestation of exile, was one of the five remaining giants at the time of King David's appearance. The original mission of God to deal with the descendants of the Nephilim would not be accomplished until one man, after God's heart stood in the face of the demonic half-breed.

The previous missions to eradicate the Nephilim from the earth were about to be concluded. This was a long-awaited moment that began with Moses, continued through Joshua, and concluded through King David and his mighty men. Moses fought battles with giants, including Sihon and Og, who were both associated with the word *Rephaim* meaning *shades* (see Deut. 3:1–8). Both Sihon and Og were recognized as Kings of the Amorites, and they were mentioned by the prophetic words of Amos, *"Yet it was I who destroyed the Amorite before them, whose height was like the height of the cedars, and he was as strong as the oaks; yet I destroyed his fruit above and his roots beneath"* (Amos 2:9).

Og, the King of Bashan, is mentioned as the remaining giant king whom Moses brought to his demise: *"For only Og king of Bashan remained of the remnant of the giants. Indeed his bedstead was an iron bedstead. (Is it not in Rabbah of the people of Ammon?) Nine cubits is its length and four cubits its width, according to the standard cubit"* (Deut. 3:11). Dr. Michael Heiser, who has done extensive work regarding the watchers and their giant offspring, writes about Og, King of Bashan, and the size of his bed being measured at thirteen feet.[6] It appears that some of the Rephaim survivors settled in Philistine territory and reemerged once again to fight against the armies of Israel.

Goliath was of the remnant of Rephaim, the angelic half-breeds whose seed agenda was to the *"bruise"* the *"heal"* of those who were of God's seed (Gen. 3:15). It was the same agenda as in the garden. Then this agenda was being carried out by Goliath. It should have been dealt with a long time before this, but Israel had neglected her call to spiritual warfare and slaying the giants. The giants were now a thorn in Israel's flesh, something Israel already had been warned of:

But if you do not drive out the inhabitants of the land from before you, then it shall be that those whom you let remain shall be irritants in your eyes and thorns in your sides, and they shall harass you in the land where you dwell.

—Numbers 33:55

The Lord spoke His plan to Israel to drive out the inhabitants of the land, the giants who occupied the promise. God had a plan, and Israel was called by God to partner in that plan. If they failed to fulfill their mission of dealing with the giants, the remaining seed of the Nephilim

75

would become a thorn in the side of the Seed of Messiah. When Paul used the language of *"a thorn in the flesh"* that was afflicting him, he called it *"a messenger of Satan"* (2 Cor. 12:7). It is not completely clear as to who or what people group he may have been talking about, but Paul was clearly using the same language as a reference to the *"seed"* of the serpent being a thorn in Israel's flesh.

FIVE SMOOTH STONES
& FIVE REMAINING GIANTS

God's people have inherited a call to slay the giants. Our battle is both celestial and terrestrial. This explains why Paul the apostle tells us, *"For we do not wrestle against flesh and blood, but against principalities, against powers, against the rulers of the darkness of this age, against spiritual hosts of wickedness in the heavenly places"* (Eph. 6:12).

About 400 years after the twelve spies went into the land and saw the sons of the Nephilim, Israel was still under threat of a terrorist giant named Goliath. This giant was not alone. There were four others like him, with each carrying out individual assignments of the enemy to keep God's people oppressed. The Philistines had given the giants asylum. As they harbored the enemies of God's people, they also used the giants to continue their seed agenda to trouble the plans and purposes of God in Israel.

Enter King David. By the time David began to make his appearance, Israel was caught in the crosshairs of a new giant, Goliath. Measuring at nine feet and nine inches, Goliath represented a colossal history between the "fallen ones" and the people of God. The agenda of these giants remains the same—separate God's people from God's land. Goliath was the embodiment of this as his name's meaning attested.

Goliath had an interesting feature within his armor. We are told, *"He had a bronze helmet on his head, and he was armed with a coat of mail, and the weight of the coat was five thousand shekels of bronze"* (1 Sam. 17:5). The *"coat of mail"* was an important feature to Goliath's armor. The Hebrew words to describe this piece of equipment are *širyôn qaśqeśet,* which can be translated to mean *body armor of scales.* The scales were a reminder of the serpent in the garden as if Goliath was paying homage to his spiritual ancestry. Goliath's ominous presence was a symbol of the historic enemy occupation in the Land of Promise, and his defeat meant everything to Israel's prophetic future. Giants did not belong in the Land of Promise. Something had to be done.

> *So the men of Israel said, "Have you seen this man who has come up? Surely he has come up to defy Israel; and it shall be that the man who kills him the king will enrich with great riches, will give him his daughter, and give his father's house exemption from taxes in Israel."*
>
> —1 Samuel 17:25

On the heels of this promise, David asked an incredibly important question about Goliath, *"What shall be done for the man who kills this Philistine and takes away the reproach from Israel? For who is this uncircumcised Philistine, that he should defy the armies of the living God?"* (v. 26). We cannot quickly pass over this statement, as if David was making this about circumcision. David knew the giant was a descendant of fallen angels and fallen giants, so the question was not just about his members, but his manhood. Goliath was not a man, and David knew it. Goliath was the seed of the serpent, and David identified the agenda of the serpent as *"reproach"* (v. 26).

Reproach is the enemy's agenda. It is the shame the serpent caused beginning in the garden when mankind took on shame and hid themselves from the presence of the Lord (see Gen. 3:7–10). Goliath was reproducing the shame, disgrace, and disappointment that had been haunting God's people from the beginning. David questioned, *"What shall be done for the man who kills this Philistine and takes away the reproach from Israel?"* (1 Sam. 17:26).

Listen to this—God wants to take away the reproach from your life. Everything that has haunted you, shamed you, tamed you, and disgraced you, the Spirit of the Living God within you wants to take down, and the bigger these things are, the harder they will fall.

It has been said that necessity is the mother of invention. Well, David was about to do something no one had ever heard of. Normally, you want to bring a gun to a knife fight, but David brought a rock. Saul, the king preceding David, attempted to place his armor and sword on David, but David was not a two-dimensional man. David was not going to win this battle with two-dimensional thinking. David was fighting a spiritual battle, and he knew it.

The clue to David's mindset about this moment was made evident when David picked up *"five smooth stones from the brook"* (1 Sam. 17:40). Why did he need five when we find out later that all David needed was one shot? David was not preparing to miss, but he was preparing for something more than Goliath. Only later do we find out what David was planning at the battle of Goliath. There were four other giants hiding out, who could have decided to make a cameo appearance and avenge Goliath's defeat. Whether it was that day or some time down the road, David took five river rocks in prophetic anticipation of Israel's destiny to fulfill God's original mandate of dealing with the giants.

As you read the *secret of the giants*, I believe you are going to begin to get language to identify the giants that have been against your life. Remember these giants are the offspring of rebellious angels. Everything they do is to sabotage the plan of God for you and your family line. The intent of these fallen beings is to get your seed mingled with theirs and co-opt your gifts for their agenda. You have to resist, but if you do not know who is stealing from you, a further injustice will take place.

There is a spiritual principle at work in this secret. If you can identify the thief and bring it before the Lord, you will recover what is lost, with interest!

> *People do not despise a thief if he steals to satisfy himself when he is starving. Yet when he is found, he must restore sevenfold; he may have to give up all the substance of his house.*
>
> —Proverbs 6:30–31

However, another spiritual principle exists when you cannot identify the thief. You may know you have been stolen from, but if you cannot identify the thief, you may find yourself in further trouble.

If a man delivers to his neighbor money or articles to keep, and it is stolen out of the man's house, if the thief is found, he shall pay double. If the thief is not found, then the master of the house shall be brought to the judges to see whether he has put his hand into his neighbor's goods.

—Exodus 22:7–8

It is not enough to realize you have been stolen from. The enemy has been working against you trying to steal your seat at the table. Do not let the enemy get away with it! It is time to recover everything that has been taken from you and get back sevenfold restoration. Now is the time to identify the thief and defeat the giants. The question is—what giants are taking from you?

There were five remaining giants hiding out in the Philistine camp. Goliath was the first to fall, and David's victory over Goliath cascaded into something bigger. When the Philistines were at war again with Israel, David's mighty men took out the other four remaining giants. These giants were physical manifestations of a spiritual reality. Each one was identified by a name that accurately described its serpent agenda.

GIANT 1. GOLIATH: EXILE

Goliath was the first to fall in this series of five. Remember, Goliath's name means *exile*. His agenda is to intimidate you into isolation, ultimately attempting to remove you from your place of promise. Just as David fought Goliath with an unknown weapon, so did Jesus. Moments after David released the rock from his sling, the rock crushed the forehead of Goliath, just as the serpent was cursed to *"eat dust"* (Gen. 3:14). Goliath fell face first to the dust of the earth with a bruised head promised by God over the serpent's seed back in the garden (see Gen. 3:15).

David did not stop there. He immediately rushed at the fallen giant without a sword in hand and cut off Goliath's head with the blade of Goliath's own sword (see 1 Sam. 17:51). What did David do with this giant demon-skull? We read, *"And David took the head of the Philistine and brought it to Jerusalem, but he put his armor in his tent"* (1 Sam. 17:54). Imagine David walking into Jerusalem carrying the head of Goliath for his trophy!

We are told that Goliath's home territory was Gath (see 1 Sam. 17:4). This Philistine city was home to the five remaining giants who threatened Israel's safety. The name *Gath* means "winepress."[7] Like grapes being crushed in a winepress, King David crushed Goliath's head, providing a turning point for Israel's success.

It is no mere coincidence that Jesus was crucified at a place called Golgotha: *"And He, bearing His cross, went out to a place called the Place of a Skull, which is called in Hebrew, Golgotha"* (John 19:17). Respected Protestant theologian, James B. Jordan writes:

> Golgotha is just a contraction of Goliath of Gath (Hebrew: Goliath-Gath). First Samuel 17:54 says that David took the head of Goliath to Jerusalem, but since Jerusalem was to be a holy city, this dead corpse would not have been set up inside the city, but someplace outside. The Mount of Olives was

right in front of the city (1 Kings 11:7; 2 Kings 23:13), and a place of ready access. Jesus was crucified at the place where Goliath's head had been exhibited. Even as His foot was bruised, He was crushing the giant's head!"[8]

It was at the same place David displayed the crushed skull of Goliath that Jesus crushed the satanic powers of the enemy upon the cross.

And you, being dead in your trespasses and the uncircumcision of your flesh, He has made alive together with Him, having forgiven you all trespasses, having wiped out the handwriting of requirements that was against us, which was contrary to us. And He has taken it out of the way, having nailed it to the cross. Having disarmed principalities and powers, He made a public spectacle of them, triumphing over them in it.

—Colossians 2:13–15

The first giant has already been disarmed by the cross of Christ. Jesus is Victor, and He has overcome the works of satan.

GIANT 2. ISHBI-BENOB: MY SEAT IS IN THE HIGH PLACE

The next giant to fall after Goliath was Ishbi-Benob. This giant tried to attack at a time when *"David grew faint,"* thinking *"he could kill David"* (2 Sam. 21:15–16).

82

When the Philistines were at war again with Israel, David and his servants with him went down and fought against the Philistines; and David grew faint. Then Ishbi-Benob, who was one of the sons of the giant, the weight of whose bronze spear was three hundred shekels, who was bearing a new sword, thought he could kill David. But Abishai the son of Zeruiah came to his aid, and struck the Philistine and killed him. Then the men of David swore to him, saying, "You shall go out no more with us to battle, lest you quench the lamp of Israel."

—2 Samuel 21:15–17

It was not David who would slay this giant, but one of David's mighty champions named Abishai. Such was Abishai's victory over this giant that, afterward, David's men forbade him from going back in to battle, concerned he might *"quench the lamp of Israel"* (v. 17). The mighty men of Israel understood something—God's spotlight was on David, and if Abishai were to continue to fight wars, he may unintentionally take the spotlight and cut short the purposes of God through King David. This is a great test. Can you have great victory without the accolades of others and yet be secure in your identity to let God choose upon whom He wants to shine His spotlight? To defeat this giant, you must be of that kind of heart.

Ishbi-Benob literally means, "My seat is at Nob."[9] The meaning of *Nob* is "high place" and is considered the priestly city where David ate the holy bread set apart only for the priests (see 1 Sam. 21:6). Nob was known as a high place, an elevated location quite possibly near the Mount of Olives.[10]

Ishbi-Benob is the giant that does not want you accessing the high places. This giant is a religious giant trying to keep you operating out of a lower spiritual level, keeping you far from the spiritual heights God is calling you to. If you have ever faced this giant, his agenda is to keep you from living in the high place that your spiritual life calls for. He is the giant that keeps you from accessing spiritual realms.

When this giant is at work, he keeps you from leveling up and stepping into a realm of supernatural miracle flow. This giant wants to take your seat at the table of the Lord and keep you from operating in your mandate as a priest in the presence of God. You cannot tolerate this religious giant. He wants to sit in the priestly high place for himself, and subtly suppresses everyone else from moving in the realm of the Spirit as a Kingdom of priests. Do not let this giant take your seat at the table of the Lord.

GIANT 3. SAPH: TALL, THRESHOLD, FENCE KEEPER

The next to fall was Saph who fell to the hand of David's champion Sibbechai: *"Now it happened afterward that there was again a battle with the Philistines at Gob. Then Sibbechai the Hushathite killed Saph, who was one of the sons of the giant"* (2 Sam. 21:18). Believed to be one of the three warriors who broke through enemy lines to obtain a drink of water for David from a well in Philistine territory, Sibbechai fought against Saph or Sippai, whose name means tall, threshold, and fence keeper (see 2 Sam. 23:16). In other words, this giant is like an invisible barrier, a glass ceiling if you will, and its goal is to keep you small. This giant has to be the tallest in the region, and it works tirelessly attempting to thwart and retaliate for any promotion placed upon you.

Tall poppy syndrome is a cultural phenomenon that tries to put down anyone whose success intimidates societal norms. Around the world, there are gifts and talents that are meant to be seen in order to inspire culture to reach for greater heights. The Spirit of the Living God has hidden this treasure in His field. The field is the world, and at the right time, God will place His finger on a person, a region, or a movement to demonstrate His greatness at work through His people. This giant's tactics are "cutting down the tall poppy" to maintain the status quo.

God wants you to bust through this invisible barrier. You may have felt this spirit try to attack you by undermining you, exploiting your inadequacies, and making you afraid to stand out. You must take authority over this giant and break through to take your place as an influencer of the culture around you. Do not shrink back in fear or hold your bright idea back anymore. God is giving you a boldness to step forward and shine like the stars. The key to victory over this giant is boldness and confidence in what God has called you to. As Daniel said, *"Those who are wise shall shine like the brightness of the firmament. And those who turn many to righteousness like the stars forever and ever"* (Dan. 12:3).

GIANT 4. LAHMI: EAT BREAD, MY BREAD, AND BREAD EATER

We find our fourth giant in First Chronicles 20:5, *"Again there was war with the Philistines, and Elhanan the son of Jair killed Lahmi the brother of Goliath the Gittite, the shaft of whose spear was like a weaver's beam."* Lahmi used similar weapons tactics as his brother Goliath. Both of them carried an unusual spear. The spear was "like a weaver's beam" (1 Sam. 17:7; 1 Chron. 20:5). The illustrative wording is used to describe the technological advantage and size this spear had beyond any other spear. Elhanan had to be a skilled warrior to dodge the spear of Lahmi. Like his mentor, King David evaded Saul when an evil spirit came upon the king, and King Saul threw the spear at David with every intention of pinning him against the wall (see 1 Sam. 19:9–10). The evil spirit that came upon Saul, turning him against David, was the same evil that Lahmi operated out of.

Lahmi's name means "bread eater," and this giant seeks to eat up your provision. I have seen this spirit, and it has an ugly desire to devour the resources God has given you. It is important to recognize that bread is often pictured as provision in the Scripture, and whenever you see this giant at work, it will try to steal your bread.

Elhanan, whose name means "God is gracious," fought against this giant and overcame him. The key to beating this giant is to feast on God's grace.

> *And God is able to make all grace abound toward you, that you, always having all sufficiency in all things, may have an abundance for every good work. As it is written: "He has dispersed abroad, He has given to the poor; His righteousness endures forever." Now may He who supplies seed to the sower, and bread for food, supply and multiply the seed you have sown and increase the fruits of your righteousness.*
>
> —2 Corinthians 9:8–10

The grace of God teaches us there is more than enough, and when the enemy tries to come against you in this area, *"Do not be overcome by evil, but overcome evil with good"* (Rom. 12:21).

GIANT 5. THE SIX-FINGERED, SIX-TOED GIANT: HEALTH ISSUES

The last giant was an unnamed monster. He could only be identified by his six toes on each foot and his six fingers on each hand. This is important because this giant carried a health issue called *polydactyly*, resulting in supernumerary excess of fingers and toes:

> *Yet again there was war at Gath, where there was a man of great stature, who had six fingers on each hand and six toes on each foot, twenty-four in number; and he also was born to the giant. So when he defied Israel, Jonathan the son of Shimea, David's brother, killed him.*
>
> —2 Samuel 21:20–21

Healing is a fundamental part of our covenant promise. This fifth giant uses sickness as a means to sabotage a move of God in your life. Just before moving into something regarding Heaven's purpose, this giant will use whatever it can throw at you to get you weakened and worn out, in a vulnerable state for attack.

Spiritual life and physical health go hand in hand. God wants to break you free from every form of sickness and disease. He also wants you to be a giant slayer and rid this world of its six-fingered grip of sickness and disease. Jesus has made a way for you to be victorious over sickness and disease: *"by whose stripes you were healed"* (1 Pet. 2:24). Just like Jesus whom God anointed *"with the Holy Spirit and with power, who went about doing good and healing all who were oppressed by the devil, for God was with Him,"* you are now anointed to slay this giant (Acts 10:38). Jesus sends you, saying, *"And heal the sick there, and say to them, 'The kingdom of God has come near to you'"* (Luke 10:9).

EPOCHAL MOMENTS

There are moments in history that are so significant they mark a transition from one era to a new era. Events like this transform the world as we know it and often make the way for a dynamic shift in culture, thus setting the stage for a new normal. The exodus out of Egypt was the defining moment for Israel's relationship with YHWH. Israel once was a person; however, when God spoke to Moses about the oppression of His people in Egypt, Israel was seen as a nation (see Exod. 3:7). Israel's cultural identity became solidified, and then she had to unlearn the Egyptian ways so as to learn what it meant to be a *"kingdom of priests and a holy nation"* (Exod. 19:6).

The events that took place at the tower of Babel were another example of an epochal moment which impacted every living person. At one moment, the world was operating out of a unified language, with no communication barriers. When God saw them operating as one and *"nothing that they propose to do* [would] *be withheld from them,"* He downloaded a language code into the system of humanity that completely transformed society from one unified language to a world separated by language and geography (Gen. 11:6).

Today's epochal moments are things ranging from the fall of the Berlin Wall, to 9–11, to the creation of the smartphone, and now the outbreak of the pandemic. Each of these moments have shifted culture and transformed the way we see and interact with the world. There are times and seasons for everything, and what initiates the change of season can be one thing or a series of little things converging in on each other to alter the current expression of what we now know.

As David reached for his sling, a series of chain reactions were set into motion, causing an epochal moment for the nation of Israel. The prophetic fulfillment of slain giants began a cultural shift, opening the doorway to move from tabernacle to temple. The next move on Heaven's time clock after the fall of the giants was when God moved His people into preparation for the temple. The original mission to deal with the Nephilim offspring of the *bēn 'ĕlōhîm* (sons of God in Gen. 6) was complete. God was now ready to move from a mobile home called *the tabernacle* to a permanent, fixed place called *the temple*.

Directly after the fall of the giants, David began to prepare the resources for a temple-building project that would become realized in his son Solomon. This would take Israel out of the age of war to an age of great glory:

> *And David said to Solomon: "My son, as for me, it was in my mind to build a house to the name of the Lord my God; but the word of the Lord came to me, saying, 'You have shed much blood and have made great wars; you shall not build a house for My name, because you have shed much blood on the earth in My sight. Behold, a son shall be born to you, who shall be a man of rest; and I will give him rest from all his enemies all around. His name shall be Solomon, for I will give peace and quietness to Israel in his days. He shall build a house for My name, and he shall be My son, and I will be his Father; and I will establish the throne of his kingdom over Israel forever.'"*
>
> —1 Chronicles 22:7–10

During this time, the rare things became common among the children of Israel. What was previously hard to find was made abundantly available in a time of uncommon glory. The children of Israel had a history where common things were rare. As they journeyed through the wilderness, the menu available was basic. But, during the time when the temple was established, the Scripture tells us, *"The king made silver as common in Jerusalem as stones, and he made cedar trees as abundant as the sycamores which are in the lowland"* (1 Kings 10:27).

Perhaps we are in an epochal moment where God wants the rare things to become common—a time of great transition from glory to glory—but the giants must be dealt with. The giants of exile and his four giant relatives must be defeated. Jesus took out Goliath at the cross. It is our time to slay the giants of sickness, the religious giants, the bread-eating giants, and the giants standing in the way, keeping God's people bound to cultural oppression. As we face these giants, we will begin to see a shift in the world around us, moving God's people into a time of great glory.

As the giants fall, rare things become common, and the things previously inaccessible become widely available. Scholarships should become common among our children. Miracles should become a common experience in our churches. Dreams and visions should be a normal aspect of our faith. God is going to use you to bring the giants down so that the rare things may become common among God's people!

KEYS TO ACTIVATING THIS SECRET

The *secret of the giants* is a powerful key being imparted to the Body of Christ. It's time to face your giants. Here are some practical steps to walking out the power of this secret.

GUARD YOUR HILL OF BEANS

As David ascended to the throne, other great leaders arose by David's side to bring Israel to a place of incredible victory. King David inspired a generation of heroes who held back nothing as they went to battle to protect the kingdom. The Scriptures speak of these mighty men who took their place in history as formidable warriors, capable of deathly feats.

Champion warriors like Benaiah, who *"killed two lion-like heroes of Moab. He also had gone down and killed a lion in the midst of a pit on a snowy day"* (2 Sam. 23:20). Or Eleazar, when everyone retreated from the battle, he *"arose and attacked the Philistines until his hand was weary, and his hand stuck to the sword"* (v. 10). Those who retreated returned after Eleazar's great victory to receive the plunder from this one-man army.

All these warriors are impressive and their stories legendary. But the one who sticks out to me the most is Shammah. He defended a hill of beans from the enemies of Israel. You may be thinking what every other Israelite was probably thinking, *It's just a hill of beans*. Right. But I want to encourage you to guard your hill of beans, no matter how insignificant anyone else may make it out to be:

> *And after him was Shammah the son of Agee the Hararite.*
> *The Philistines had gathered together into a troop where*
> *there was a piece of ground full of lentils. So the people fled*
> *from the Philistines. But he stationed himself in the middle of*
> *the field, defended it, and killed the Philistines. So the Lord*
> *brought about a great victory.*
>
> —2 Samuel 23:11–12

Do not let the giants take your hill. Defend what others are too afraid to defend. God will give you a good name.

SPEAK TO YOUR GIANTS

Identify the giants you have been facing. How is the enemy standing in the way of the land God has called you to inherit? Write out the giants opposing you by their names, and begin to make the declaration that Joshua and Caleb did when they saw the giants dwelling in their land of promise. Speak this word as a declaration.

> *If the Lord delights in us, then He will bring us into this land and give it to us, 'a land which flows with milk and honey.' Only do not rebel against the Lord, nor fear the people of the land, for they are our bread; their protection has departed from them, and the Lord is with us. Do not fear them.*
>
> —Numbers 14:8–9

Make a declaration like King David did when Goliath cursed David, but David responded with a prophetic declaration:

> *Then David said to the Philistine, "You come to me with a sword, with a spear, and with a javelin. But I come to you in the name of the Lord of hosts, the God of the armies of Israel, whom you have defied. This day the Lord will deliver you into my hand, and I will strike you and take your head from you. And this day I will give the carcasses of the camp of the Philistines to the birds of the air and the wild beasts of*

*the earth, that all the earth may know that there is a God in
Israel. Then all this assembly shall know that the Lord does
not save with sword and spear; for the battle is the Lord's, and
He will give you into our hands."*

—1 Samuel 17:45–47

NOTES

1. The Abraham Lincoln Institute for the Study of Leadership and Public Policy, "Lincoln at Niagara Falls," September 28, 2013, https://lincolninstitute.wordpress.com/2013/09/28/lincoln-at-niagara-falls.

2. Hugh Ross, *Navigating Genesis: A Scientist's Journey through Genesis 1–11* (Covina, CA: RTB Press, 2014), 130, Kindle.

3. Ross, *Navigating Genesis*, 130.

4. Ross, *Navigating Genesis*, 131.

5. Nickelsburg and VanderKam, *1 Enoch*, 24–25.

6. https://www.biblestudymagazine.com/bible-study-magazine-blog/when-giants-walked.

7. *Strong's Hebrew Lexicon (NKJV)*, s.v. "H1661 gaṯ," https://www.blueletterbible.org/lexicon/h1661/nkjv/wlc/0-1.

8. James B. Jordan, *Biblical Horizons Newsletter* 84, "Christ in the Holy of Holies The Meaning of the Mount of Olives" (April, 1996).

9. *Strong's Hebrew Lexicon (NKJV)*, s.v. "H3430—yišḇô bᵉnōḇ," https://www.blueletterbible.org/lexicon/h3430/nkjv/wlc/0-1.

10. *BibleHub*, s.v. "Nob," https://bibleatlas.org/full/nob.htm.

CHAPTER 4

THE SECRET OF
THE CHERUBIM

*Then I looked, and behold, a whirlwind was coming out of the
north, a great cloud with raging fire engulfing itself; and brightness
was all around it and radiating out of its midst like the color
of amber, out of the midst of the fire. Also from within it came
the likeness of four living creatures. And this was their
appearance: they had the likeness of a man. Each one
had four faces, and each one had four wings.*

—Ezekiel 1:4–6

*I am convinced that these heavenly beings exist and that they
provide unseen aid on our behalf. I do not believe in angels because
someone has told me about a dramatic visitation from an angel,
impressive as such rare testimonies may be. I do not believe in angels
because UFOs are astonishingly angel-like in some of their reported
appearances. I do not believe in angels because ESP experts are
making the realm of the spirit world seem more and more plausible.
I do not believe in angels because of the sudden world-wide emphasis
on the reality of satan and demons. I do not believe in angels because
I have ever seen one, because I haven't. I believe in angels because
the Bible says there are angels, and I believe the Bible to be the
true Word of God. I also believe in angels because I have
sensed their presence in my life on special occasions.*

—Billy Graham[1]

SECRETS OF THE ANGELS

I had come home from some time away, back to my folks' house where I grew up. It was Christmas, and keeping with Christmas tradition, we watched *It's a Wonderful Life*. It is an oldie but a goodie that was originally shown in black and white. Watching it made me feel as if I went back in time. The main character, George Bailey, endures a series of setbacks, leading him to a point in his life where he does not want to go on any longer. On Christmas Eve, George contemplates suicide and finds himself in a rescue attempt from an angel named Clarence. Clarence has been given a mission to save George Bailey in order to get his wings.

The angel Clarence takes George on a curious journey of visions, showing him what the world would be like without George Bailey in it. The message hit George loud and clear. Begging Clarence to get his life back, everything returns to the way it was. George rushes home to wake up his family. While George embraces his family with his little daughter Zuzu in his arms, George looks down to see a new copy of *The Adventures of Tom Sawyer* by Mark Twain. Intrigued, George opens to find a handwritten note on the inside of the cover, saying, "Dear George: Remember, no man is a failure who has friends. Thanks for the wings! Love Clarence." Just then, a bell rings that had been hung on the nearby Christmas tree. George's little daughter Zuzu exclaims, "Look, Daddy, every time a bell rings an angel gets his wings!"

It had been almost a year since I had been at my parents' home. My travels had taken me to quite a few places around the world, but as the saying goes, "There is no place like home." That night, I planned to get some good sleep and wake up the next morning to go to church with my folks. I found a good couch to lay on, wrangled up a blanket, smuggled a pillow out of a nearby bedroom, and went to bed. I quickly fell asleep.

About the middle of the night, I woke up to a noise. It was a song, but I could not understand the words. It was a beautiful song though otherworldly. Startled by the song, I opened my eyes, hoping to understand where this song was coming from. As I opened my eyes, I looked up, and there standing in front of me was an angelic creature that was quite tall. The fear of the Lord came upon me, but the song seemed to comfort me at the same time. The angelic being did not look like anything I could imagine. It had the face of an eagle with feathers that looked like they were made of silver. I was mesmerized by what I was seeing.

The being was not talking, only singing in a language I could not understand. I could feel my physical body being recharged by the power of the song. What happened next, the only way I can describe it, was as if I felt like my feet were being washed. In that place, I felt a peace I had never experienced before. It was overwhelming. As the angelic being continued singing, I fell back asleep as if it were singing me into a spirit of a deep sleep.

Waking up the next morning, I was undone by what I had seen and experienced. I could still feel the same peace I had felt while the angelic being was singing its song. Stranger still, I could still feel what I felt in my feet after they had been washed.

Now, you might be wondering what I ate that night before bed! Or, you may have already checked out and said, "Okay, this stuff ain't for me." Or, you may be like me, intensely seeking to find out more about Heaven and the realm of angels. Well, if you are willing to wander dangerously into the things of God, keep reading! This is the *secret of the cherubim*!

DO ANGELS HAVE WINGS?

Now it is easy to assume all angels have wings. Paintings like the great Leonardo da Vinci's *Annunciation* depict the angel Gabriel with spectacular wings, kneeling before Mary to announce the miraculous conception of Christ. Perhaps you have seen the little angel cherubs with wings pictured in *The Madonna of San Sisto* by Raphael. Angels have been the interest of many for centuries, but the lifelike art of the Renaissance has imprinted upon us what an angel should look like, wings and all. But the question we should be asking is this: Do all angels have wings?

The Scriptures are full of stories of angels. Some have the resemblance of men and others have the resemblance of a human with wings. Some have the resemblance of women with wings *"like a stork"* (Zech. 5:9). Still others have multiple pairs of wings. What are we to make of this?

The presumption is that if you are a flying being from Heaven you must have wings. Wings help you to fly, right? Well, the problem is that the Scripture fails to mention evidence of wings on many of the angelic appearances. When Abraham received the Lord as his honored guest, the angelic beings standing with the Lord are described as *"men"* (Gen. 18:2). However, when Ezekiel sees the vision of the cherubim, *"Each one had four faces and each one four wings, and the likeness of the hands of a man was under their wings"* (Ezek. 10:21). There is an oddity about these cherubim when comparing them to other angelic-like beings who are more human in appearance in the Scripture; the cherubim seem to have animal-like features mixed with human-like features. These are hybrid beings that seem to have a story of their own.

CHERUBIM

There are two distinct categories of these type of animal-like beings in heaven, cherubim and seraphim. Ezekiel had multiple visionary encounters wherein he described cherubim playing a key role in the heavenly experiences. Ezekiel had a vision of them: *"Their legs were straight, and the soles of their feet were like the soles of calves' feet. They sparkled like the color of burnished bronze"* (Ezek. 1:7). The animal-like characteristics cannot be missed. There are certain aspects of the cherubim of Ezekiel's vision that are shared in common with the four living creatures from the apostle John's vision in Revelation 4 and 5.

THE FACES OF EZEKIEL'S FOUR LIVING CREATURES.

As for the likeness of their faces, each had the face of a man; each of the four had the face of a lion on the right side, each of the four had the face of an ox on the left side, and each of the four had the face of an eagle.

—Ezekiel 1:10

THE FACES OF REVELATION'S FOUR LIVING CREATURES.

The first living creature was like a lion, the second living creature like a calf, the third living creature had a face like a man, and the fourth living creature was like a flying eagle.

—Revelation 4:7

The lion, eagle, ox, and man theme is a shared similarity between these two distinguishable groups. One of the unique differences about the living creatures of Ezekiel's vision when comparing them to the four living creatures is the number of their faces. While the four living creatures of Revelation have four unique faces, the four living creatures of Ezekiel's vision have four unique faces on each of the four. Four sets of faces on the four cherubim give us sixteen faces among them.

Interestingly, the four distinct face types correspond to the four cardinal points of the Babylonian zodiac.[2] Remember, Ezekiel is a Babylonian captive during the time of these visions. Some could say God was using the language of the culture where Ezekiel was living. Others could say the Babylonian culture saw something of Heaven accurately. Either way, the vision is communicating something. God is in charge of all time. The characters of the Babylonian zodiac represent times and seasons, and God is King over all time, even the determined time of Israel's captivity in Babylon.

The constellations of the zodiac are not something we should be afraid to talk about. Why? Because the heavens declare God's glory! However, those constellations are for something far superior than some strange zodiac reading about your horoscope. Quit that! The Scripture clearly warns about this saying,

You are wearied in the multitude of your counsels; let now the astrologers, the stargazers, and the monthly prognosticators stand up and save you from what shall come upon you.
—Isaiah 47:13

The constellations are for *"signs and for seasons"* (Gen. 1:14). By the way, those constellations are not actually called the zodiac. God identified them by another name called *Mazzaroth*, simply meaning *constellations*, and He alone is the sovereign Ruler of their orbit. Even Job was reminded by God of the sovereign rule He has over these heavenly bodies:

Can you bind the cluster of the Pleiades, or loose the belt of Orion? Can you bring out Mazzaroth in its season? Or can you guide the Great Bear with its cubs? Do you know the ordinances of the heavens? Can you set their dominion over the earth?

—Job 38:31–33

The constellations are a reminder to us of the story of God. This is why some Jewish synagogues depict illustrative imagery of the Mazzaroth constellations with God's chariot throne at the center (e.g., Beit Alpha).[3] They are a display of His Kingdom message, reminding us that God is the supreme Ruler over all time and can do with time what He wills! King David caught the same revelation, writing, *"You have hedged me behind and before, and laid Your hand upon me. Such knowledge is too wonderful for me; it is high, I cannot attain it"* (Ps. 139:5–6).

The other distinguishable difference of the Ezekiel's cherubim is where and when they are seen. The four living creatures seem to move in tandem with wheels that are intended to give us a picture of a chariot throne:

The appearance of the wheels and their workings was like the color of beryl, and all four had the same likeness. The appearance of their workings was, as it were, a wheel in the middle of a wheel. When they moved, they went toward any one of four directions; they did not turn aside when they went. As for their rims, they were so high they were awesome; and their rims were full of eyes, all around the four of them.

—Ezekiel 1:16–18

The idea of a chariot throne was not foreign to the prophets. The prophet Daniel recorded a vision of the Ancient of Days, writing, *"I watched till thrones were put in place, and the Ancient of Days was seated; His garment was white as snow, and the hair of His head was like pure wool.* **His throne was a fiery flame, its wheels a burning fire***"* (Dan. 7:9). Even the instructions for constructing the ark of the covenant contain the required imagery of a chariot: *"And refined gold by weight for the altar of incense, and for the construction of* **the chariot, that is, the gold cherubim** *that spread their wings and overshadowed the ark of the covenant of the Lord"* (1 Chron. 28:18).

The wheels also play a significant part in the scenery of the vision. They are described as being four sets of a wheel within a wheel.

And when I looked, there were four wheels by the cherubim, **one wheel by one cherub and another wheel by each other cherub***; the wheels appeared to have the color of a beryl stone. As for their appearance, all four looked alike—as it were,* **a wheel in the middle of a wheel***. When they went, they went toward any of their four directions; they did not turn aside when they went, but followed in the direction the head was facing. They did not turn aside when they went. And their whole body, with their back, their hands, their wings, and the*

102

*wheels that the four had, were full of eyes all around. As for
the wheels, they were called in my hearing, "Wheel."*

—Ezekiel 10:9–13

The wheels seem to have a connection to a corresponding cherub.
The wheels are locked into the cherubim's movements as if they were
synchronized.

*When the living creatures went, the wheels went beside them;
and when the living creatures were lifted up from the earth,
the wheels were lifted up. Wherever the spirit wanted to go,
they went, because there the spirit went; and the wheels were
lifted together with them, for the spirit of the living creatures
was in the wheels. When those went, these went; when those
stood, these stood; and when those were lifted up from the
earth, the wheels were lifted up together with them, for the
spirit of the living creatures was in the wheels.*

—Ezekiel 1:19–21

The imagery of the four living creatures as representations of times and
seasons in sync with the wheel within the wheel begins to make sense
when we understand what the wheel is portraying. The wheel can be
likened to an astronomical instrument called *an astrolabe*.[4] Such an
instrument was used as a multipurpose astronomical tool for reckoning
time. An instrument of this type would be capable of helping measure
the time of year, measure the time of the night, measure the time of
the day, measure the position of celestial objects, and many other
important uses, making this an incredibly important tool. Think of it an
astronomical model of the universe that was small enough to be held in
the palm of your hand.

By now, you should be connecting the dots. God rules over all time, and He can chart times and seasons like a captain on the high seas. Yahweh is the sovereign Ruler over all the cosmos, and He is the One *"who holds the seven stars in His right hand"* (Rev. 2:1). The cherubim are cosmic attendants to His sovereign administration over the timeline of all things. The chariot and cherubim are not some sort of heavenly contraption, like God's time machine. Ezekiel was witnessing the Sovereign Lord, in the fullness of glory, demonstrating His supreme authority over time.

There is no coincidence as to the timing of this revelation to the prophet Ezekiel. Israel had been carried off into Babylonian captivity, and you can imagine the difficulty Israel was having believing God's promises. When the God of Israel appeared to Ezekiel who was among the captives on the banks of the Chebar River, the Israeli refugees were at the beginning of what may have seemed to them to be a permanent exile. However, God as the Ruler of time was about to reveal to Ezekiel that all of time is in His hands.

> *Then I looked, and behold, a whirlwind was coming out of the north, a great cloud with raging fire engulfing itself; and brightness was all around it and radiating out of its midst like the color of amber, out of the midst of the fire. Also from within it came the likeness of four living creatures. And this was their appearance: they had the likeness of a man.*
>
> —Ezekiel 1:4–5

REDEEMING TIME

The *secret of the cherubim* is a revelation of God's majesty over time. He can stop time like He did with Joshua when the *"sun stood still, and the moon stopped, till the people had revenge upon their enemies"* (Josh. 10:13). He can turn back time like He did when He added fifteen more years to Hezekiah's life, giving him a sign through the prophet Isaiah.

> *"And this is the sign to you from the Lord, that the Lord will do this thing which He has spoken: Behold, I will bring the shadow on the sundial, which has gone down with the sun on the sundial of Ahaz, ten degrees backward." So the sun returned ten degrees on the dial by which it had gone down.*
>
> —Isaiah 38:7–8

When the Scriptures speak of the timing of God, it is not fatalistic. Time is in His hands. As Habakkuk wrote concerning God's timing, *"For the vision is yet for an appointed time, but at the end it will speak, and it will not lie. Though it tarries, wait for it; because it will surely come, it will not tarry"* (Hab. 2:3).

Under God's redemptive authority, time can be accelerated, and He can give you a harvest so abundant that it makes up for any time that was lost.

> *"Behold, the days are coming," says the Lord, "When the plowman shall overtake the reaper, and the treader of grapes him who sows seed; the mountains shall drip with sweet wine, and all the hills shall flow with it. I will bring back the captives of My people Israel; they shall build the waste cities and inhabit them; they shall plant vineyards and drink wine from them; they shall also make gardens and eat fruit from*

them. I will plant them in their land, and no longer shall they be pulled up from the land I have given them," says the Lord your God.

—Amos 9:13–15

REVERSE THE CURSE

Dreams are one of the primary ways God uses to speak to me by His Spirit. I write about this in my book *Secrets of the Seer*. I have a whole chapter diving into this subject; it's called, "The Secret of Dreams." I have learned that the more I pay attention to my dreams, the more often I have them, and if I write them down, the more often I can easily remember them. Some dreams can often feel like they are written in disappearing ink. You may think you can remember them, but as time goes on, the message fades. However, some dreams stick with you in a way that may completely shift your thinking. The following is one of those dreams for me.

The dream began where I found myself in the back of a big, long bus. I was all the way back and could look out the back window to the road moving away from us. I was enjoying the ride when, all the sudden, my attention was drawn to the bus driver. He looked like he had a little grin on his face, and I could see him all the way up in the front driving while I was in the far back.

In the dream, the bus driver turned, looked at me, and said, "Hey, watch this!" The driver immediately pulled on the gear shift and put the bus in reverse. I was alarmed but intrigued by his behavior. Almost immediately, we were at top speed in reverse. I turned back around to look out the back and nervously watched as we moved through a very narrow pathway in reverse at top speed! Miraculously, we did not run into anything. Though there were tight boundaries on both sides of the road, the driver was able to keep us in reverse at top speed without any damage done!

A moment later, the dream continued, but this time I was on a train. Once again, I was all the way at the back of a very long train. The train was moving extremely fast, and I was looking out the back at all the train tracks we just crossed over. Suddenly, it was as if I had Superman vision giving me the ability to see at a greater distance. From the back, I could see the conductor all the way at the front. He was driving the train, making sure everything was going smoothly. In that moment, something caught my attention. He looked very familiar to me. I could not see his face because his back was toward me, but he would turn his head just enough that his profile looked like someone I had seen before somewhere else.

Suddenly, the conductor turned around and looked right at me with a big grin on his face. It was the bus driver! He stared at me with a giant grin and said, "Hey, watch this!" Instantly, he put the train in reverse and headed backwards down the train track at top speed. Again, I nervously looked out the window of the back, this time worried we were going to derail. And just as with the bus, the conductor perfectly navigated the train in reverse at top speed.

Here is the thing: God is about to put things in REVERSE! Some big things are about to be reversed in your life! I was in the far back of both the bus and the train, but because the movement was in reverse, what seemed like the backseat was actually the front row for the acceleration

SECRETS OF THE ANGELS

in reverse! If you have felt like you have been in the back row, God is offering you a front row seat as He accelerates the reversal of things that felt too big to reverse! He will keep you on track on His time as He turns the clock back!

When I woke up from the dream, a big grin came over my face. I knew the conductor in the dream was the Lord. The picture of His big grinning face looking at me made me chuckle.

TIMES & SEASONS ARE NOT A CURSE

The *secret of the cherubim* reveals to us that God is the supreme Ruler over all time! Every timeline is perfectly calculated. As Daniel said,

> *Blessed be the name of God forever and ever, for wisdom and might are His. And He changes the times and the seasons; He removes kings and raises up kings; He gives wisdom to the wise and knowledge to those who have understanding. He reveals deep and secret things; He knows what is in the darkness, and light dwells with Him.*
>
> —Daniel 2:20–22

The cherubim assist God in navigating His redemptive plan through the power of times and seasons. So, it is time for us to allow our understanding of times and seasons to level up.

On Noah's six-hundred-and-first birthday, the waters began to dry up. For a little over a year, Noah and his family had not stepped foot on dry ground. When the ark finally opened and they were able to step out of the ark, Noah built an alter to offer a burnt offering.

> *And the Lord smelled a soothing aroma. Then the Lord said in His heart, "I will never again curse the ground for man's sake, although the imagination of man's heart is evil from his youth; nor will I again destroy every living thing as I have done. While the earth remains, seedtime and harvest, cold and heat, winter and summer, and day and night shall not cease."*
>
> —Genesis 8:21–22

The Lord said, *"Never again will I curse the ground for man's sake"* (v. 21). He then made a promise, guaranteeing *"seedtime and harvest, cold and heat, winter and summer, and day and night"* (v. 22). Think of it this way: The curse is a lack of seasons while the promise is the blessing of the seasons. God wants to reverse the curse in your life and your family, but He wants you to begin partnering with Him for times and seasons.

King Solomon identified twenty-eight unique times and seasons in his book, Ecclesiastes. He begins with, *"To everything there is a season, a time for every purpose under heaven"* (Eccl. 3:1). It is vital to know the time and season God has placed you in. I find it extremely telling that the curse of not obeying the voice of the Lord will be, *"In the morning you shall say, 'Oh, that it were evening!' And at evening you shall say, 'Oh, that it were morning!' because of the fear which terrifies your heart, and because of the sight which your eyes see"* (Deut. 28:67). The *secret of the cherubim* is the revelation that God is the sovereign Administrator of all timelines and He can teach you how to lean into His voice for your season.

KEYS TO ACTIVATING THIS SECRET

The *secret of the cherubim* is a powerful key, giving us a glimpse into the angelic realms' participation in the Lord's sovereign administration of time. It's time to get your time back. Here are some practical steps to walking out the power of this secret.

REMEMBER THE SABBATH

Remembering the Sabbath is the first key to redeeming your time.

> *If you turn away your foot from the Sabbath, from doing your pleasure on My holy day, and call the Sabbath a delight, the holy day of the Lord honorable, and shall honor Him, not doing your own ways, nor finding your own pleasure, nor speaking your own words, then you shall delight yourself in the Lord; And I will cause you to ride on the high hills of the earth, and feed you with the heritage of Jacob your father. The mouth of the Lord has spoken.*
>
> —Isaiah 58:13–14

Sabbath may mean different things to different people. As Paul wrote, *"One person esteems one day above another; another esteems every day alike. Let each be fully convinced in his own mind"* (Rom. 14:5). However, in the spirit of the Sabbath, the meaning to us is simple. Christ is our Sabbath, and *"There remains therefore a rest for the people of God"* (Heb. 4:9).

The *secret of the cherubim* reminds us of the power of rest. When Ezekiel saw the vision of the cherubim, the Israelites had been carried into Babylonian captivity because they had failed to let the ground Sabbath (see 2 Chron. 36:21). Every seven years the people of Israel were commanded to let the ground rest and observe a Sabbath to the Lord (see Lev. 25:4). God would provide more than enough during the sixth year leading up to the seventh so they could have enough for three years! He gave them this promise, saying:

> *And if you say, "What shall we eat in the seventh year, since we shall not sow nor gather in our produce?" Then I will command My blessing on you in the sixth year, and it will bring forth produce enough for three years. And you shall sow in the eighth year, and eat old produce until the ninth year; until its produce comes in, you shall eat of the old harvest.*
>
> —Leviticus 25:20–22

Because they had lacked trust in God's provision, they stole from God and did not rest in the seventh year. Trusting God means acknowledging our time is in His hands. When you commit your time to His purpose, you will see success! *"Commit your works to the Lord, and your thoughts will be established"* (Prov. 16:3).

Take an assessment of the time you set apart to practice God's presence. Become intentional about giving Him your time. When you do, you are redeeming your time and recalibrating your time to eternity. Right now, begin to ask the Holy Spirit for supernatural instructions for a day of Sabbath rest. By faith, enter the rest by dedicating a day unto the Lord and trusting Him with your time.

But as for me, I trust in You, O Lord; I say, "You are my
God." My times are in Your hand; deliver me from the hand of
my enemies, and from those who persecute me.

—Psalm 31:14–15

SPEAK OVER YOUR TIME

Time is voice activated; the very fabric of time was spoken into existence. Joshua, for example, spoke over his time. He said, *"Sun, stand still over Gibeon; and Moon, in the Valley of Aijalon"* (Josh. 10:12). Then we read that *"the sun stood still and the moon stopped, till the people had revenge upon their enemies"* (v. 13).

When you speak over your time, you are activating a realm of angelic breakthrough. You are like Ezekiel, calling to the four winds, when the Spirit of God spoke to him, saying, *"Prophesy to the breath, prophesy, son of man, and say to the breath, 'Thus says the Lord God: "Come from the four winds, O breath, and breathe on these slain, that they may live"'"* (Ezek. 37:9). You are like Joshua, speaking to the sun and moon, to time itself. Take back your time and speak over it, that you may see great victory!

Pray this prayer with me:

Lord, You are the sovereign Administrator of all time. The
cherubim surround You, and there is no time outside of Your
authority. My times and seasons are in the palm of Your hand.
Take Your place as the Lord of my timeline. Let the cherubim

assist You in the sovereign rule of time, and may all the
angels and saints praise You as the Alpha and the Omega, the
Beginning and the End. Amen.

NOTES

1. Billy Graham, *Angels: God's Secret Agents* (Nashville: Thomas Nelson, 1995), chap. 1.

2. Dr. Michael S. Heiser, "Ezekiel's Vision, Part 2," *Dr. Michael S. Heiser* (blog), August 17, 2008, https://drmsh.com/ezekiels-vision-part-2.

3. *BibleWalks*, s.v. "Beit Alpha—Ancient Synagogue and Zodiac Mosaic, https://www.biblewalks.com/beitalpha.

4. Karen Meech, "Astrolabe History," *University of Hawaii Institute for Astronomy*, April 18, 2000, https://www.ifa.hawaii.edu/tops/astl-hist .html.

CHAPTER 5

THE SECRET OF THE SERAPHIM

In the year that King Uzziah died, I saw the Lord sitting
on a throne, high and lifted up, and the train of His robe
filled the temple. Above it stood seraphim; each one had six
wings: with two he covered his face, with two he covered his feet,
and with two he flew. And one cried to another and said: "Holy, holy,
holy is the Lord of hosts; The whole earth is full of His glory!"

—Isaiah 6:1–3

All that is sweet, delightful, and amiable in this world, in the
serenity of the air, the fineness of seasons, the joy of light,
the melody of sounds, the beauty of colors, the fragrancy of smells,
the splendor of precious stones, is nothing else but Heaven
breaking through the veil of this world.

—William Law[1]

In Isaiah's vision, the word *seraphim* described the angelic-like beings surrounding God's throne. The word used to identify the winged-like beings is found in the Hebrew root word, *śārāp̄* ("serpent"). This word has been sometimes understood as coming from the root word, *śārap* ("to burn"). However, studies have shown it is more likely linked to the word, *śārāp̄* ("serpent").[2] The seraphim would have been imagined to

SECRETS OF THE ANGELS

be closely symbolic of a flying serpent-like creature with the wings of a cobra and the venom of a fiery dragon. This should cause lightbulbs to go off in your head when we discuss the serpent in the garden of Eden.

Dr. Michael Heiser explores the subject of serphim in his book, *Angels*, writing,

> As I noted in *The Unseen Realm*, "It is more likely that seraphim derives from the Hebrew noun śārap ("serpent"), which in turn is drawn from Egyptian throne guardian terminology and conceptions." As recent research demonstrates, the Egyptian Uraeus serpent, drawn from two species of Egyptian cobras, fits all the elements of the supernatural seraphim who attend Yahweh's holy presence in Isaiah 6.[3]

The seraphim are not considered angels as the word for angel in Hebrew, *mal'āk*, is not used to identify these heavenly beings.[4] Unlike angels who often are sent on missions as messengers, seraphim are stationed at the throne as divine throne guardians. The throne guardian imagery begins to really make sense when you consider the showdown of the serpents in the account of Moses at Pharoah's court.

Moses instructed his brother, Aaron, "*When Pharaoh speaks to you, saying, 'Show a miracle for yourselves,' then you shall say to Aaron, 'Take your rod and cast it before Pharaoh, and let it become a serpent'*" (Exod. 7:9). When Moses and Aaron stepped into Pharaoh's court and did as they were commanded by God, the magicians of Egypt, the sorcerers, and all of Pharaoh's best performed their sorcery to challenge the serpent of Aaron's rod. *"For every man threw down his rod, and they became serpents. But Aaron's rod swallowed up their rods"* (v. 12).

I hope you are connecting the dots. We may have a commonly held preconception telling us, "Serpent is bad." But we have to understand that it was God who commanded Moses to cast down his staff.

> *So the Lord said to him, "What is that in your hand?" He said, "A rod." And He said, "Cast it on the ground." So he cast it on the ground, and it became a serpent; and Moses fled from it. Then the Lord said to Moses, "Reach out your hand and take it by the tail" (and he reached out his hand and caught it, and it became a rod in his hand), "that they may believe that the Lord God of their fathers, the God of Abraham, the God of Isaac, and the God of Jacob, has appeared to you."*
>
> —Exodus 4:2–5

God was about to make one of the biggest moves in all of Israel's history. How did He start it out? He began with an epic battle of throne guardians. It was as if He was prophetically portraying to Egypt that the throne of Pharaoh was about to be breached and there would only be one victor. Yahweh.

COALS FROM THE ALTAR

Isaiah's eyes were opened to see the throne of God with seraphim standing around Him. And there the Lord sat, *"high and lifted up, and the train of His robe filled the temple"* (Isa. 6:1) The vision was illustrating something incredibly powerful about the Lord. He is the King over every other king.

In those days, a king who defeated the opposing king would cut off the defeated king's train to have it sewn onto the train of his robe. The king would sit in an elevated place so that the train of his robe would have space. In Solomon's day, the throne itself had six steps (1 Kings 10:19). The text does not explicitly say it was for King Solomon's robe; however, you can imagine it was a perfect setting for the train of the king's robe.

Have you ever been to a live concert and sat near the speaker system during the show? If the speaker systems are loud enough, you can feel the vibrations of soundwaves coming out of the speakers and bouncing off your chest. As Isaiah was caught up in the realm of glory, he heard one of the seraphim crying out to another, *"Holy, holy, holy is the Lord of hosts; the whole earth is full of His glory!"* (v. 3).

We are told the sound of the seraphim's voices was so powerful that *"the posts of the door were shaken by the voice of him who cried out, and the house was filled with smoke"* (v. 4). The intensity of what Isaiah saw made him come undone. He wrote, *"So I said: 'Woe is me, for I am undone! Because I am a man of unclean lips, and I dwell in the midst of a people of unclean lips; for my eyes have seen the King, the Lord of hosts"* (v. 5).

Gripped by the weight of iniquity that came from his own mouth, one of the seraphim flew to Isaiah with a burning coal taken by tongs from the altar: *"And he touched my mouth with it, and said: 'Behold, this has touched your lips; your iniquity is taken away, and your sin purged'"* (Isa. 6:7).

There is so much happening here that needs to be unpacked. The key to understanding what is happening here is the power of sacred space. Isaiah had just been caught up in the realm of God's sacred space, the place of absolute holiness. Isaiah's calling only came after the coal touched Isaiah's lips, cleansing him from the iniquity of his culture and thereby qualifying him to be set apart as a representative of the realm of sacred space. Then he heard *"the voice of the Lord, saying, 'Whom shall I send, and who will go for Us?' Then I said, 'Here am I! Send me'"* (v. 8).

SACRED SPACE

The seraphim are guardians of the sacred space where God dwells. They administrate the coals from the altar. The allegorical lamentation for the king of Tyre contains what many scholars believe is the story of Lucifer's fall.

> *Son of man, take up a lamentation for the king of Tyre, and say to him, "Thus says the Lord God: 'You were the seal of perfection, full of wisdom and perfect in beauty. You were in Eden, the garden of God; every precious stone was your covering: the sardius, topaz, and diamond, beryl, onyx, and jasper, sapphire, turquoise, and emerald with gold. The workmanship of your timbrels and pipes was prepared for you on the day you were created. **You were the anointed***

cherub who covers; I established you; you were on the holy
mountain of God; you walked back and forth in the midst of
fiery stones. You were perfect in your ways from the day you
were created, till iniquity was found in you.'"

—Ezekiel 28:12–15

The divine rebel had access to walk *"in the midst of fiery stones"* until iniquity was found in him, no longer giving him access to the sacred space of *"the holy mountain of God"* (v. 14). However, the reverse is true with Isaiah. The moment Isaiah saw the Lord, and recognized his own iniquity and the iniquity of his people, the coals of the altar, the fiery stones touched his lips, cleansing him, and giving him the ability to represent the sacred space of God's presence!

Moses also came into contact with the realm of God's sacred space. When the Lord revealed Himself to Moses, a warning came from God's presence, saying, *"Do not draw near this place. Take your sandals off your feet, for the place where you stand is holy ground"* (Exod. 3:5). When we read of this moment, we cannot mistakenly perceive God's warning to Moses as God trying to push Moses away. No! God was trying to invite him into a deeper realm of connection, the realm of sacred space. And He was teaching Moses how to think about the sacred dwelling of God's presence.

Whenever I am a guest at someone else's house, I always check first if I should take my shoes off before entering. No need to bring the stuff of the outside to the floor on the inside. However, Moses was not being taught a lesson on hygiene. This was a realm of sacred space, and God wanted Moses to get in touch with it. Yahweh asked Moses to take off

THE SECRET OF THE SERAPHIM

his sandals, not only to honor the sacredness of the space, but to get Moses' feet connected to holy ground with nothing in-between.

Touching sacred space is not something to be taken lightly. When you touch sacred space, a chain reaction can occur and completely alter your state of being. To some it can cause adverse reactions, while others experience it as new life. When Uzzah reached out his hand to stabilize the ark, he took hold of it, and it seemed to have shocked his system. The text shows how serious this was, telling us, *"Then the anger of the Lord was aroused against Uzzah, and God struck him there for his error; and he died there by the ark of God"* (2 Sam. 6:7).

UNVEILED FACE

For the believer, the transformative power of the glory of the sacred space is the revelation of the unveiled face. I call it, *sacred space, unveiled face*. When God invites you into a realm of sacred space, the glory of God transforms you to live in the glory of an unveiled face.

> *But we all, with unveiled face, beholding as in a mirror the glory of the Lord, are being transformed into the same image from glory to glory, just as by the Spirit of the Lord.*
> —2 Corinthians 3:18

When Moses was commanded to take off his sandals in the sacred space of God's glory, it began a transformative work in Moses, setting him apart to be a prophetic representative commissioned by God. As Moses led the children of Israel out of Egypt, Moses was then called up to Mount Sinai for forty days in the presence of the God of glory. When coming down from the mountain, the children of Israel saw something they had never seen before.

> *Now it was so, when Moses came down from Mount Sinai (and the two tablets of the Testimony were in Moses' hand when he came down from the mountain), that Moses did not know that the skin of his face shone while he talked with Him.*
>
> —Exodus 34:29

The skin of Moses' face was shining with glory, but he did not realize it. He had been sitting with God for forty days, in the place of sacred space. Not even food or water touched his lips for forty days as He spoke with God in the cloud (see Exod. 34:28). God's presence in that sacred space was the Bread from Heaven and the Living Water. Moses shone with God's glory.

When Moses returned to the children of Israel, they could not handle his shining face. I can hear them saying, "Put your mask on Moses!" Or, "You're not wearing it right." Whatever they said, Moses did not speak to the children of Israel without a mask when he would declare to them what he heard in the place of sacred space (Exod. 34:33). However, when he went into God's presence at the tabernacle of meeting, he would take off the mask and see God with an unveiled face.

And like the seraphim who used their wings to cover their faces, Moses had to cover his face with a veil. But God wants to lift the veil off your face. God wants to give you the *secret of the seraphim—sacred space with unveiled face.*

FACE OF A MAN, EAGLE, LION, OX

John the beloved, called by many as Jesus' best friend while on Earth, was the disciple who Jesus entrusted to care for and look after Jesus' mother, Mary. While John was on the Isle of Patmos, exiled by Rome to a prison island, he received *The Revelation of Jesus Christ*. The book of Revelation has been a book of wonder and mystery for many for close to two millennia. The opening paragraph is my favorite part.

> *The Revelation of Jesus Christ, which God gave Him to show His servants—things which must shortly take place. And He sent and signified it by His angel to His servant John, who bore witness to the word of God, and to the testimony of Jesus Christ, to all things that he saw. Blessed is he who reads and those who hear the words of this prophecy, and keep those things which are written in it; for the time is near.*
>
> —Revelation 1:1–3

John heard the voice from heaven calling, *"Come up here, and I will show you things which must take place after this"* (Rev. 4:1). Like Isaiah's vision of the *"Lord sitting on a throne, high and lifted up,"* John was caught up into a rare glimpse of the throne room of Heaven (Isa. 6:1). *"One sat on the throne. And He who sat there was like a jasper and a sardius stone in appearance; and there was a rainbow around the throne, in appearance like an emerald"* (Rev. 4:2–3).

SECRETS OF THE ANGELS

A familiar song can be heard that is much like the seraphim's song in Isaiah's vision. Four living creatures are before the throne, *"And they do not rest day or night, saying: 'Holy, holy, holy, Lord God Almighty, Who was and is and is to come!'"* (Rev. 4:8). The seraphim in Isaiah's vision have a similar cadence to their song. *"And one cried to another and said: 'Holy, holy, holy is the Lord of hosts; the whole earth is full of His glory!'"* (Isa. 6:3).

Unlike the cherubim who have a total of four wings each, the four living creatures have a total of six wings matching the number of the wings of the seraphim (Ezek. 1:6). *"The four living creatures, each having six wings, were full of eyes around and within"* (Rev. 4:8). However, in Isaiah's vision, we are only given a glimpse of who these seraphim were. Two of their wings were used to cover their face, two to cover their feet, and two to fly (see Isa. 6:2). The veil of wings in Isaiah's encounter was lifted when John saw the throne of the "One." The flying throne guardians were no longer covering their faces. They had unveiled faces from the sacred space of God's throne of glory! It was hidden from the eyes of Isaiah, but to John the beloved apostle, they were seen with their faces revealed.

> *The first living creature was like a lion, the second living*
> *creature like a calf, the third living creature had a face like*
> *a man, and the fourth living creature was like a flying eagle.*
> *The four living creatures, each having six wings, were full of*
> *eyes around and within. And they do not rest day or night,*
> *saying: "Holy, holy, holy, Lord God Almighty, who was and is*
> *and is to come!"*
>
> —Revelation 4:7–8

What was it that changed everything for them? What could give them permission to lift the veil off their eyes? Well, even the heavens themselves were impure from the lies spoken of by the enemy. In Isaiah's prophetic proclamation of judgment on the enemy, the prophecy contains a description of five lies that were spoken in the heavens. These are known as the five "I will" statements.

> *How you are fallen from heaven, O Lucifer, son of the*
> *morning! How you are cut down to the ground, you who*
> *weakened the nations! For you have said in your heart: "I*
> *will ascend into heaven, I will exalt my throne above the stars*
> *of God; I will also sit on the mount of the congregation on*
> *the farthest sides of the north; I will ascend above the heights*
> *of the clouds, I will be like the Most High." Yet you shall be*
> *brought down to Sheol, to the lowest depths of the Pit.*
>
> —Isaiah 14:12–15

The heavens themselves felt the effect of those five lies. The Scripture speaks of those who joined the enemy in his divine rebellion, saying, *"And the angels who did not keep their proper domain, but left their own abode, He has reserved in everlasting chains under darkness for the judgment of the great day"* (Jude 1:6). The heavens needed a cleansing, and Christ is the offering made once for all the cosmos, to cleanse the earth and the heavens. The enemy polluted the heavens with his five lies, but Jesus has cleansed the heavens by the power of His sacrifice.

> *Therefore it was necessary that the copies of the things in*
> *the heavens should be purified with these, but the heavenly*

things themselves with better sacrifices than these. For Christ has not entered the holy places made with hands, which are copies of the true, but into heaven itself, now to appear in the presence of God for us.

—Hebrews 9:23–24

It was the cross of Christ and the power of His resurrection that lifted the veil off the eyes of things in Heaven and on Earth! Therefore, because of Christ's offering for all, we can come into the presence of God with an unveiled face. We no longer need to approach the presence in a replica of the tabernacle that is a copy of the things in the heavenly realm. We can boldly approach the throne of grace, into the throne room of Heaven, with full assurance and an unveiled face.

Therefore, brethren, having boldness to enter the Holiest by the blood of Jesus, by a new and living way which He consecrated for us, through the veil, that is, His flesh, and having a High Priest over the house of God, let us draw near with a true heart in full assurance of faith, having our hearts sprinkled from an evil conscience and our bodies washed with pure water. Let us hold fast the confession of our hope without wavering, for He who promised is faithful.

—Hebrews 10:19–23

The *secret of the seraphim* is the *unveiled face in sacred space*. If the skin of Moses' face was shining from the presence of God, what does your face look like as you boldly approach the sacred space where God dwells?

KEYS TO UNLOCKING THIS SECRET

The *secret of the seraphim* is a powerful key giving us a glimpse into the realities of sacred space. God wants to give you the power and an unveiled face. Here are some practical steps to walking out the power of this secret.

GIVE GOD SACRED SPACE

Giving God sacred space means dedicating a place to meet with Him, hear from Him, and worship Him. Moses had such a place. He pitched his tent *"outside the camp, far from the camp, and called it the tabernacle of meeting. And it came to pass that everyone who sought the Lord went out to the tabernacle of meeting which was outside the camp"* (Exod. 33:7).

Where is your tent of meeting? It does not have to be an elaborately decorated space. It is simply a place of sacred space for you to have communion with God. Angels may join you there! You may see visions of the throne like the prophet Isaiah and John the beloved did! Give God a place where He knows He can meet you. For Moses, it was the tent of meeting. For Jesus, it was the Mount of Olives. Find the place where you experience the presence of God and protect that place. It is sacred.

Like the seraphim who dwell in sacred space with an unveiled face, offer your space to the Holy Spirit, and He will make your face shine!

Those who are wise shall shine like the brightness of the firmament, and those who turn many to righteousness like the stars forever and ever.

—Daniel 12:3

FACE OF AN ANGEL

When the disciple Stephen spoke with boldness about the majesty of Jesus, those who looked upon him, *"saw his face as the face of an angel"* (Acts 6:15). However, the apostle Paul said that the *"gospel is veiled . . . to those who are perishing, whose minds the god of the age has blinded, who do not believe"* (2 Cor. 4:3–4). The veil that rests over the eyes, over the mind, and over the heart, however, is lifted as we turn to meet God where He is. The Spirit of the Lord is lifting the veil and giving us an ability to see Him like never before. It's about turning to meet with Him. *"Nevertheless when one turns to the Lord, the veil is taken away"* (2 Cor. 3:16).

When we get caught up in the moment and get our eyes off the majesty of Jesus, we have allowed the veil back over the eyes of our hearts. When we lose focus on the presence of God, we begin to lose our ability to see. Angels are at work, but we have lost our sensitivity to the spiritual world, and we cannot tell what Heaven is up to. When we turn to the Lord and value His presence, the veil is lifted, and our faces shine as the faces of angels.

Pray this prayer with me:

Lord, remove the veil from my heart. Let the eyes of my heart be unmasked to see You like the seraphim see You. Let my face shine with Your glory that others may look and see Your glory upon me. Let my face shine like the face of an angel as I look to You! Amen.

NOTES

1. William Law, *An Appeal to All Doubt, The Works of the Reverend William Law*, Vol. VI (London: Robinson and Roberts, 1762), 116–117.

2. Philippe Provençal, "Regarding the Noun שרף in the Hebrew Bible," *Journal for the Study of the Old Testament*, vol. 29, no. 3, Mar. 2005, 371–379, https://doi.org/10.1177/0309089205052683.

3. Dr. Michael S. Heiser, *Angels: What the Bible Really Says about God's Heavenly Host* (Bellingham, WA: Lexham Press, 2018), chap. 1.

4. *Strong's Hebrew Lexicon* (KJV), s.v. "H4397—mal'āk," https://www.blueletterbible.org/lexicon/h4397/kjv/wlc/0-1.

CHAPTER 6

THE SECRET OF THE ARCHANGELS

*Yes, while I was speaking in prayer, the man Gabriel, whom
I had seen in the vision at the beginning, being caused to
fly swiftly, reached me about the time of the evening offering.
And he informed me, and talked with me, and said, "O Daniel,
I have now come forth to give you skill to understand."*

—Daniel 9:21–22

*Thou hast seen His power, which is in all the world; tarry now
no longer upon earth, but ascend on high. Ascend, I say, in
imagination even unto the first heaven, and behold there so
many countless myriads of Angels. Mount up in thy thoughts,
if thou canst, yet higher; consider, I pray thee, the Archangels,
consider also the Spirits; consider the Virtues, consider the
Principalities, consider the Powers, consider the Thrones,
consider the Dominions—of all these the Comforter is the
Ruler from God, and the Teacher, and the Sanctifier.*

—Saint Cyril of Jerusalem[1]

I had been traveling for over twenty-four hours, making my way to
Indonesia. For the next five days, I would be spending time praying

and ministering to the wonderful people from many of the different surrounding regions of Asia. I remember looking out the window as our vehicle climbed higher and higher through the Puncak Pass. It was early enough to see the mist of fog hovering over the surrounding greenery, but I could still see people out on the mountain walking through the beautiful landscape. I asked the guide what they were out doing, walking so early in the morning through the fields on the mountain.

"Harvesting tea," he responded.

We continued our drive through the forest of tea leaves, higher up Indonesia's highest mountain peak.

Arriving at the location of the meetings, I was thrilled to have been given immediate access to a room with a bed. On the other side of the world, my body was still adapted to U.S. time. I desperately needed to get a quick sleep in before taking in the breathtaking beauty of this place.

I got into my room and found the bed and immediately fell asleep. It was so fast that, when I started dreaming, I still thought I was awake. I could not tell the difference and thought I was somehow still awake because the dream began with me still on the mountain walking around and taking in the majesty of it all.

Suddenly, in the dream, I heard a loud voice proclaim, "An archangel from Heaven has come to Earth!" The voice could only be described as something the Scripture calls, *"a loud voice, as of a trumpet"*

(Rev. 1:10). Immediately, the appearance of something like lightning was near me on my side. It was too quick for me to look at because something else burst through the sky. It was the Lord, and He was as big as the sky itself, flying upon the clouds, like imagery from the blessing of Moses, *"There is no one like the God of Jeshurun, Who rides the heavens to help you, and in His excellency on the clouds"* (Deut. 33:26). Yahweh is the Cloud Rider, and I could not take it all in as it felt like I had to turn my head because my eyes could not turn far enough to take in His Majesty.

I could not see His face. I could see glimpses of His face, but it was as if clouds were moving all across His face so as to cover certain aspects of it while revealing other aspects of it. I could not look away. In that moment, frozen, staring at what I was seeing, the only thing I could think of was, "You're like big giant, Jesus!" The writer of Hebrews explains this mystery so well.

> *God, who at various times and in various ways spoke in time past to the fathers by the prophets, has in these last days spoken to us by His Son, whom He has appointed heir of all things, through whom also He made the worlds; who being the brightness of His glory and the express image of His person, and upholding all things by the word of His power, when He had by Himself purged our sins, sat down at the right hand of the Majesty on high.*
>
> —Hebrews 1:1–3

Jesus is the exact expression of the image of the Father. When the disciple Philip asked Jesus to take them behind the curtain and see the Father who had been instructing Jesus to do miraculous works, Jesus responded, *"Have I been with you so long, and yet you have not known Me, Philip? He who has seen Me has seen the Father; so how can you say, 'Show us the Father'?"* (John 14:9). To look upon Jesus is to look upon the Father. However, the same is true of the Father! When you see the Father, it will be like looking upon Jesus!

Waking up, I sat up out of bed, stunned by what I had just been privileged to see. I could only worship.

About an hour later, my friend Samuel Robinson stopped by my room to connect. He had just traveled from Canada, and we were both scheduled to speak that week at the meetings. We shared stories and got to catch up and began to share with each other what the Holy Spirit had been speaking to us about the upcoming meetings. As Sammy and I shared with each other the messages God had given to us, I shared with Sammy the dream I had just awoken from about an hour earlier.

Something shifted in that room while I shared the dream. We could feel the atmosphere shift, and what felt like the glory of God came into that place. I felt heat was being applied to my face, like when a blow dryer hits the skin of your face, and it warms your whole body. My face was feeling the intensity of the glory of God.

Sammy jumped up out of his seat and began walking frantically back and forth in front of me. I asked him, "Are you okay?"

He looked stunned and pointed at my face and said, "Bro, you are glowing!" Apparently, my face was glowing like the top of a Christmas tree!

Later that night, the meetings kicked off with our host, Rev. Dr. Jedidiah Tham. As the worship wrapped up, Dr. Tham moved us into a time of ministering the Word. Sammy and I sat down where we were seated, and Jedidiah began to speak, "During worship, I saw an archangel from Heaven being sent to this place!" Sammy just about fell out of his seat in shock as he turned around staring at me, trying to wrap his mind around what had just happened.

THE ARCHANGELS OF HEAVEN

You may be asking what the difference is between an angel and an archangel. There are very few direct references to archangels in the text. In the Old Testament, we read about certain named angels, but it gives very little insight as to their ranking among other angels. In the New Testament, we are given a little more insight into their ranking and their roles.

While there are multiple instances of angels mentioned in the Scripture, only three of two of them are named, Michael and Gabriel. Their association with each other comes from the mention of their initial reveal in the same passage of Scripture. Later in the New Testament, Michael is identified as an archangel (Jude 1:9). The book of Daniel is the first to have identified these archangels, and their appearances happen throughout the prophetic visions of Daniel's prophecy.

Archangels are distinct from the other angels for their ranking is superior. When Daniel received the visitation toward the end of a twenty-one-day fast, the Messenger who had been sent told Daniel the story of his delay.

135

Then he said to me, "Do not fear, Daniel, for from the first
day that you set your heart to understand, and to humble
yourself before your God, your words were heard; and I have
come because of your words. But the prince of the kingdom of
Persia withstood me twenty-one days; and behold, Michael,
one of the chief princes, came to help me, for I had been left
alone there with the kings of Persia. Now I have come to make
you understand what will happen to your people in the latter
days, for the vision refers to many days yet to come."

—Daniel 10:12–14

Daniel gave himself to a twenty-one-day fast, today known as the "Daniel fast," searching to understand the times and seasons. The supernatural being giving this message had to fight through demonically occupied territory. He had been withstood by the prince of Persia for twenty-one days, the length of this time corresponding with the warfare Daniel was struggling through in his own flesh as he humbled himself before God.

The message given revealed angelic support was necessary to break through the opposition from the prince of Persia. While the prince of Persia was called a prince, a title to recognize this principality, the archangel Michael, who supported Heaven's purpose to reveal to Daniel this message, was called *"one of the chief princes"* (Dan. 10:13). Archangels are distinguished as "chief princes," giving them a ranking higher than that of other angels. Though they are identified as "chief princes," it should be noted they are not the chief prince as in the chief prince over all others, but a chief prince among others like them. The authority they represent comes from one higher in rank, *"the Prince of princes"* (Dan. 8:25). This dynamic

136

is clear when you look at Daniel's visitation by the angel Gabriel, who was speaking on behalf of the voice of someone else standing by—someone who had *"a man's voice between the banks of the Ulai, who called, and said, 'Gabriel, make this man understand the vision'"* (Dan. 8:17). It is apparent that archangels work under the leadership of the Prince of princes.

THE MAN CLOTHED IN LINEN

When Gabriel made his first appearance, he was not alone. Though the archangel had approached Daniel, he was not speaking to Daniel until he was instructed to speak by the voice of another standing by (Dan. 8:16–17). This was further explored at the end of Daniel's epic prophecy of the future when the mysterious man in Daniel's vision was accompanied by two others inquiring of *"the man clothed in linen"* (Dan. 12:6). We read,

> *Then I, Daniel, looked; and there stood two others, one on this riverbank and the other on that riverbank. And one said to the man clothed in linen, who was above the waters of the river, "How long shall the fulfillment of these wonders be?" Then I heard the man clothed in linen, who was above the waters of the river, when he held up his right hand and his left hand to heaven, and swore by Him who lives forever, that it shall be for a time, times, and half a time; and when the power of the holy people has been completely shattered, all these things shall be finished.*

> —Daniel 12:5–7

The man clothed in linen was not named, but the appearance of the man clothed in linen was curiously detailed earlier in Daniel's vision. Unlike Gabriel and Michael, who were not given any detailed explanation as to their appearances, the man clothed in linen was revealed to Daniel in spectacular glory:

> *Now on the twenty-fourth day of the first month, as I was by the side of the great river, that is, the Tigris, I lifted my eyes and looked, and behold, a certain man clothed in linen, whose waist was girded with gold of Uphaz! His body was like beryl, his face like the appearance of lightning, his eyes like torches of fire, his arms and feet like burnished bronze in color, and the sound of his words like the voice of a multitude.*
>
> —Daniel 10:4–6

This man clothed in linen was the same man who was strengthened by the archangel Michael in the heavenly war opposing the journey to give Daniel a message. He was also the one who strengthened Michael in a time of great difficulty.

> *But I will tell you what is noted in the Scripture of Truth. (No one upholds me against these, except Michael your prince. Also in the first year of Darius the Mede, I, even I, stood up to confirm and strengthen him.)*
>
> —Daniel 10:21–11:1

Who was this unnamed messenger? Daniel described his vision of the man calling him *"one having the likeness of the sons of men"* (Dan.

10:16). This is no doubt a reference to the Son of Man, seen by John on the Isle of Patmos, as he received the Revelation of Jesus Christ:

> *Then I turned to see the voice that spoke with me. And having turned I saw seven golden lampstands, and in the midst of the seven lampstands One like the Son of Man, clothed with a garment down to the feet and girded about the chest with a golden band. His head and hair were white like wool, as white as snow, and His eyes like a flame of fire; His feet were like fine brass, as if refined in a furnace, and His voice as the sound of many waters; He had in His right hand seven stars, out of His mouth went a sharp two-edged sword, and His countenance was like the sun shining in its strength. And when I saw Him, I fell at His feet as dead. But He laid His right hand on me, saying to me, "Do not be afraid; I am the First and the Last. I am He who lives, and was dead, and behold, I am alive forevermore. Amen. And I have the keys of Hades and of Death."*
>
> —Revelation 1:12–18

The *"man clothed in linen"* of Daniel 10:5, the *"one having the likeness of the sons of men"* of Daniel 10:16, is the *"Prince of princes"* mentioned in Daniel 8:25. He is the fourth man in the fire protecting Daniel's three friends who were thrown into the furnace for their refusal to worship Nebuchadnezzar or forsake faithfulness to Yahweh. The man clothed in linen is the Christ, the express image of the Living God of Hebrews 1:3, surrounded by archangels, worshiped by myriads, and revealed to us, Christ Jesus!

Then King Nebuchadnezzar was astonished; and he rose in haste and spoke, saying to his counselors, "Did we not cast three men bound into the midst of the fire?" They answered and said to the king, "True, O king." "Look!" he answered, "I see four men loose, walking in the midst of the fire; and they are not hurt, and the form of the fourth is like the Son of God."

—Daniel 3:24–25

THE VOICE OF AN ARCHANGEL

It is important for us to understand that archangels are the primary messengers who usher in the manifest presence of Jesus. We have explored examples of this from the prophet Daniel's visions. We can also see this in the advent of the new covenant. Who made the announcement to Mary of the immaculate conception? It was done by Gabriel, the archangel (see Luke 1:26). Who announced the forerunner to Jesus, the one who would be known as John the Baptist? It was Gabriel, the archangel (see Luke 1:19). Do you see the pattern here? The pattern will continue even at the fullness of Christ's coming.

For this we say to you by the word of the Lord, that we who are alive and remain until the coming of the Lord will by no means precede those who are asleep. For the Lord Himself will descend from heaven with a shout, with the voice of an archangel, and with the trumpet of God. And the dead in Christ will rise first. Then we who are alive and remain shall be caught up together with them in the clouds to meet the Lord in the air. And thus we shall always be with the Lord. Therefore comfort one another with these words.

—1 Thessalonians 4:15–18

THE SECRET OF THE ARCHANGELS

Jesus will descend to Earth with the voice of an archangel at the last trumpet. It is not clear as to whether this will be an archangel accompanying Jesus or the voice of the Lord will make a sound like that of an archangel. The Revelation of Jesus Christ contains such a moment, and there are unmistakable similarities to that of the man clothed in linen.

In Revelation, there are multiple instances where the Lord is distinguished by what is on His head and what He holds.

1. Jesus revealed with *"head and hair . . . white like wool, as white as snow"* while holding in *"His right hand seven stars"* (Rev. 1:14, 16).

2. Jesus revealed as a Lamb, *"having seven horns and seven eyes, which are the seven Spirits of God sent out into all the earth"* (Rev. 5:6). The Lamb with horns and eyes comes before the throne to take the *"scroll out of the right hand of Him who sat on the throne"* with the authority the break its seals (Rev. 4:7; Rev. 5:9).

3. Jesus revealed seated on a white cloud as *"One like the Son of Man, having on His head a golden crown, and in His hand a sharp sickle"* (Rev. 14:14).

4. Jesus revealed as *"Faithful and True,"* riding a white horse *"and on His head were many crowns"* (Rev. 19:11–12). He holds a *"sharp sword"* coming from His mouth and rules the nations with a rod of iron (Rev. 19:15).

Each of these glimpses of Christ are hard to miss as the text uses language with clear references pointing to Jesus. However, the mighty angel coming down from Heaven can be missed as a possible reference to the Angel of Yahweh.

I saw still another mighty angel coming down from heaven, clothed with a cloud. And a rainbow was on his head, his face was like the sun, and his feet like pillars of fire. He had a little book open in his hand. And he set his right foot on the sea and his left foot on the land, and cried with a loud voice, as when a lion roars. When he cried out, seven thunders uttered their voices. Now when the seven thunders uttered their voices, I was about to write; but I heard a voice from heaven saying to me, "Seal up the things which the seven thunders uttered, and do not write them."

—Revelation 10:1–4

This should not be mistaken for any normal angel. His head is covered with a rainbow, and a little book is being held. His voice is like the voice of an archangel, *"as when a lion roars."* He is so gigantic that He can only be clothed with the clouds, and He has the ability to place one foot in the sea and one foot on dry land. And there is something else that happens, reminding us of the man clothed in linen speaking to Daniel.

*Then I heard **the man clothed in linen**, who was above the waters of the river, when he **held up his right hand and his left hand to heaven**, and swore by Him who lives forever, that it shall be for a time, times, and half a time; and when the power of the holy people has been completely shattered, all these things shall be finished.*

—Daniel 12:7

The angel whom I saw standing on the sea and on the land
raised up his hand to heaven and swore by Him who lives
forever and ever, who created heaven and the things that are
in it, the earth and the things that are in it, and the sea and the
things that are in it, that there should be delay no longer, but
in the days of the sounding of the seventh angel, when he is
about to sound, the mystery of God would be finished, as He
declared to His servants the prophets.

—Revelation 10:5–7

In both instances, the heavenly messenger is pictured as holding His hands up to Heaven, and the messenger *"swore by Him who lives forever"* (Dan. 12:7; Rev. 10:5). Who is this angel? Shouldn't we have seen him throughout the Scriptures?

THE ANGEL OF YAHWEH

As Moses was making his way through the wilderness while shepherding his father-in-law's sheep, something caught his attention. A bush was burning, and the Scripture tells us, *"The Angel of the Lord appeared to him in a flame of fire from the midst of a bush"* (Exod. 3:2). To Moses however, the burning bush did not look like the Angel of the Lord; it appeared to him as a bush on fire. Moses, intrigued by what he saw, said, *"I will now turn aside and see this great sight, why the bush does not burn"* (Exod. 3:3).

As Moses drew near, a voice came to him emanating from within the bush, *"'Moses, Moses,' and Moses said, 'Here I am'"* (Exod. 4:4). The account tells us it was the voice of God that came from within the bush. God spoke to Moses:

143

Moreover He said, "I am the God of your father—the God of Abraham, the God of Isaac, and the God of Jacob." And Moses hid his face, for he was afraid to look upon God.

—Exodus 3:6

Who was speaking here? Was it God or the angel of God? The answer is, yes. The Angel of the Lord has a distinguishing quality that is different than that of the other angels. Yahweh said to His servant Moses and to the children of Israel, *"Behold, I send an Angel before you to keep you in the way and to bring you into the place which I have prepared. Beware of Him and obey His voice . . . for My name is in Him"* (Exod. 23:20–21). The Angel of the Lord bears the name of Yahweh!

When the Angel of the Lord spoke to Hagar, assuring her, *"Behold, you are with child, and you shall bear a son,"* the text tells us, *"Then she called the name of the Lord who spoke to her, You-Are-the-God-Who-Sees; for she said, 'Have I also here seen Him who sees me?'"* (Gen 16:11, 13). The Scripture identifies the messenger as the Lord, and Hagar identified Him as *"Him who sees me"* (Gen. 16:13).

Our understanding of interplay among the Trinity is given language throughout the New Testament, but the examples of the Trinity at work abound throughout the Old Testament. It was upon this foundation of biblical examples that modern apostolic theology was formed. John the disciple of Jesus, wrote, *"For there are three that bear witness in heaven: the Father, the Word, and the Holy Spirit; and these three are one"* (1 John 5:7). John was not creating some new idea. He was giving language to something known!

Samson the judge of Israel was born to a couple who could not conceive. Manoah and his wife were visited by the Angel of Yahweh, who promised them a son. Manoah asked the Angel of the Lord, *"What is Your name, that when Your words come to pass we may honor You?"* (Judg. 13:17). I love the response given to this question, *"And the Angel of the Lord said to him, 'Why do you ask My name, seeing it is wonderful?'"* (v. 18). His name is Wonderful, and we know Him by name, Jesus!

For unto us a Child is born, unto us a Son is given; and the government will be upon His shoulder. And His name will be called Wonderful, Counselor, Mighty God, Everlasting Father, Prince of Peace.

—Isaiah 9:6

When Samson's father realized who he had just seen, he had a mind melt, but it happened after the Angel stopped visiting him. At times, you see this dynamic when an angel, an archangel, and even the Angel of the Lord appeared that only afterward do those they visited realize it was an angel.

When the Angel of the Lord appeared no more to Manoah and his wife, then Manoah knew that He was the Angel of the Lord. And Manoah said to his wife, "We shall surely die, because we have seen God!"

—Judges 13:21–22

TUG OF WAR

The prophet Daniel tapped into something that reveals the way Heaven responds to the words we speak.

Then he said to me, "Do not fear, Daniel, for from the first day that you set your heart to understand, and to humble yourself before your God, your words were heard; and I have come because of your words."

—Daniel 10:12

Daniel set his heart to understand and to humble himself before God. When he did, his words became so irresistible Heaven itself went into battle to get to Daniel.

Someone once said, "Heaven is voice activated"! Getting your word heard in Heaven is a big deal!

Words win spiritual battles. When Daniel put his heart before the Lord, his words were heard, sending the Angel of the Lord into immediate action. As we know from our previous discussion, there was a battle for twenty-one days in the spiritual realm. On day one, the Lord moved into action to deliver to Daniel a prophetic answer. However, it was not until the end of Daniel's time of fasting and prayer that the Angel of the Lord arrived. What was He doing for twenty-one days? What was happening in the realm of the Spirit? Well, the Angel of the Lord definitely did not stop for coffee on His twenty-one-day journey!

Something else was going on in the unseen realm. The Angel of the Lord clarified for Daniel this seeming delay:

> *But the prince of the kingdom of Persia withstood me twenty-one days; and behold, Michael, one of the chief princes, came to help me, for I had been left alone there with the kings of Persia. Now I have come to make you understand what will happen to your people in the latter days, for the vision refers to many days yet to come.*
>
> —Daniel 10:13–14

You may have heard a preacher tell you about the spiritual war that is happening right now in the unseen realm. We are in the middle of a spiritual battle, and it is not just a war—it is a *tug of war*. Daniel had just engaged in a tug of war. While Daniel was in the natural dimension, he learned to be a spiritual man, giving him the ability to move Heaven on this side of Earth. This is the secret of activating the archangels of Heaven! I like to say that you can't push a rope; you can only pull it. Too often, we are trying to push our way into breakthrough. However, if you want to partner with the realm of angels to see Heaven break through, learn how to pull your miracle through prayer. Engaging in the tug of war through prayer is the key to partnering with the angelic powers of Heaven, angels and archangels.

Think of it this way. What is pulling on you? Is something pulling you in life or taking you in a direction you feel is inevitable? What has more pull on your life? It can be Heaven, or is something distracting you, pulling you away from Heaven's purpose for the time and season you are living in? Something can only be pulling on you when you are tethered to it. So, what are you tethered to?

The Scriptures illustrate our connection to Christ in the heavenly realm as a ship above the sea tethered to an anchor deep beneath the sea. The anchor keeps the ship from being pulled by the wind and current. We have this same anchor in the heavenly realm.

> *This hope we have as an anchor of the soul, both sure and steadfast, and which enters the Presence behind the veil, where the forerunner has entered for us, even Jesus, having become High Priest forever according to the order of Melchizedek.*
>
> —Hebrews 6:19–20

Jesus instructed Peter to cast his line into the water and pull up the first fish, saying, *"And when you have opened its mouth, you will find a piece of money"* (Matt. 17:27). Peter had to pull on something from a different realm! Like pulling something from deep water to the surface, Daniel's prayers pulled on someone deep from the heavenly realm, bringing his breakthrough to the surface of the earth! It's time for you to activate the power of your prayers to pull on Heaven.

KEYS TO UNLOCKING THIS SECRET

It is important for us to understand the key elements that increased Daniel's pull during the twenty-one-day tug of war. He was pulling on heaven for a word, partnering his faith with God's ability, and it moved the unseen realm. The posture of his heart combined with the power of his words made Daniel's prayer move Heaven like an ox pulling the weight of the plow. Here are some keys to unlocking the *secret of the archangels* and partnering with the angelic realm for a God-sized breakthrough.

PRAYERS THAT PULL

Prayers that pull are prayers that are effective at accelerating the breakthrough.

> *The effective, fervent prayer of a righteous man avails much. Elijah was a man with a nature like ours, and he prayed earnestly that it would not rain; and it did not rain on the land for three years and six months. And he prayed again, and the heaven gave rain, and the earth produced its fruit.*
>
> —James 5:16–18

The reverse is also true. There are prayers that are ineffective and seem to evaporate into thin air without producing rain. Jesus warned us about this when He identified the pointless religious behavior of mantras. *"And when you pray, do not use vain repetitions as the heathen do. For they think that they will be heard for their many words"* (Matt. 6:7).

Elijah called down fire from Heaven with prayers that pull. Daniel, Hannah, King David, the apostles, and many more found the secret to operating in the supernatural realm. They understood the tug of war. Pulling on Heaven begins in the heart. Daniel humbled himself and set his heart to understand. This kind of heart posture is like adding rocket fuel to your prayer, accelerating your spoken word into orbit.

OPEN THY MOUTH

Open thy mouth! There is power in what you say in the presence of God. It is one thing to pray with your mind; it is another thing to pray with your mouth. Job 22:28 tells us, *"You will also declare a thing, and it will be established for you; so light will shine on your ways."*

Your mouth is a gateway for the supernatural things of God. When the Spirit of the Lord is present, your declaration activates the realm of angels! If you do not know what to say, God says, *"I am the Lord your God, who brought you out of the land of Egypt; open your mouth wide, and I will fill it"* (Ps. 81:10).

When in doubt, open thy mouth! Call the rain! Angels are waiting to hear God's word come out of your mouth: *"Bless the Lord, you His angels, who excel in strength, who do His word, heeding the voice of His word"* (Ps. 103:20).

Pray this prayer with me:

> *Like Peter pulling a coin from the fish's mouth, I pull on my miracle from the realm of the Spirit to the surface of the earth. Lord, let Your word come quickly to me through Your messenger angels. Let nothing hinder the message. In the*

presence of the Lord and the presence of His angels, I declare a breakthrough that no power or principality can hinder. Send help from Your sanctuary, Lord of hosts.

NOTES

1. Cyril of Jerusalem, *On the Article, And in One Holy Ghost, the Comforter, Which Spake in the Prophets*, Lecture XVI, 23, 121, emphasis added, https://www.ccel.org/ccel/schaff/npnf207.ii.xx.html.

CHAPTER 7

THE SECRET OF THE TONGUES OF ANGELS

I know a man in Christ who fourteen years ago—whether in the body I do not know, or whether out of the body I do not know, God knows—such a one was caught up to the third heaven. And I know such a man—whether in the body or out of the body I do not know, God knows—how he was caught up into Paradise and heard inexpressible words, which it is not lawful for a man to utter.

—2 Corinthians 12:2–4

The limits of my language mean the limits of my world.

—Ludwig Wittgenstein[1]

In the sci-fi movie *Arrival*, Amy Adams plays a linguistics professor, tasked with the unusual responsibility of deciphering the language of alien visitors from another world. The problem of the language barrier is taken to another level as Adam's character, Dr. Louise Banks, enters into a planet-saving mission to understand the strange visitors from another dimension. As Banks attempts to decode the first set of messages from the alien visitors and the purpose of their arrival, two words become clear, "Offer Weapon." Banks is not convinced of this working translation and realizes the aliens are trying to actually say something less threatening, "Offer Tool." What is this tool?

The plot twist in the movie happens when Dr. Banks realizes that the tool being offered is not the type of advanced weaponry you and I might think of; the tool is the language itself. The language of the aliens alters the human perception of time as a linear concept, enabling the learner to transcend time and experience memories of future events. Imagine that! Dr. Banks uses this newly understood language to perceive the future and use that knowledge of the future to avoid a global catastrophe.

The stuff of sci-fi, right? Well, the human imagination may be more spiritual than we realize. The wild ideas portrayed in movies explore some part of our human existence in a way that makes us think beyond the natural word; these ideas are imagined in literature, movies, music, and many other various forms of artistic expression. This all may seem imaginative at first, but what was once sci-fi has become a reality.

Take Jules Verne's classic novel, *Twenty Thousand Leagues Under the Sea*. It told of a story of an electric submarine, ninety years before it was actually invented. And in *2001: A Space Odyssey*, Arthur C. Clarke described a digital newspaper called a "newspad." The 1968 classic's vision of a digital future would finally be realized on January 27, 2010, when Steve Jobs walked out on stage with the first edition ipad.[2] There are many other similar examples like these, where what was once only imagined as science fiction, has now become science fact. It is only a matter of time until thoughts become reality.

The world is changing, and the way we communicate is changing with it. As of this very moment, there are 7,139 recognized languages in the world.[3] This number is always changing. Even technology is changing the way we communicate. The language of emoji's may not be a recognized language, yet emojis are a technological way of communicating our thoughts and feelings to the world around us. How many of you did not know how to exactly say what you wanted to say in text, but a tiny little emoji face came to the rescue? Emojis are different in that they break the language barrier as the first universal form of communication post Babel.

BABEL

It can be difficult to imagine, but at one point, there was no such thing as the language barrier. Before Babylon, the entire human race was of one language. Because of the universal language, there was no limitation as to what could be accomplished. The symbol of the people's profound unity would be an infamous universal building project called the tower of Babel, *"a tower whose top is in the heavens"* (Gen 11:4). This moment is the first account where the Scriptures tell us, *"The Lord came down"*:

But the Lord came down to see the city and the tower which the sons of men had built. And the Lord said, "Indeed the people are one and they all have one language, and this is what they begin to do; now nothing that they propose to do will be withheld from them."

—Genesis 11:5–6

What could be so wrong with a building project like this? Well, God recognized the power of the unity of the people, and if they could do this, they could do anything they set their minds to do. The key supporting this unity was a universal language that empowered them with limitless possibilities. God had to come up with something before humanity set out on a unified path leading to self-destruction. So, God said,

> *"Come, let Us go down and there confuse their language, that they may not understand one another's speech." So the Lord scattered them abroad from there over the face of all the earth, and they ceased building the city. Therefore its name is called Babel, because there the Lord confused the language of all the earth; and from there the Lord scattered them abroad over the face of all the earth.*
>
> —Genesis 11:7–9

God had "an ace up His sleeve." Like a programmer introducing new code into preexistent software, God dispersed a code into humanity's frontal lobes, causing a universal change to how they communicated. No longer were they speaking in a universally understand language. The Lord had downloaded a new code into man's software and thus crippled a global agenda. The difficulty of the new languages put an end to the building project, but there it stood as Babel, a tower whose name literally means confusion.

TONGUES OF MEN & TONGUES OF ANGELS

Years ago, I had been taken into a heavenly encounter in what seemed to be in some kind of tunnel of light, only this tunnel was going straight up! I could feel the sensation as if a heavenly force was taking me higher and higher through this tunnel of light. My eyes were opened, and what I saw was light passing before my eyes. It was stunning.

As I was pulled higher and higher, I heard a sound as if a conversation was happening all around me. The only thing I could understand was my name. It was the angels of God speaking to one another in a language I had never heard before. They were speaking, and I could tangibly feel God's glory intensifying every time they spoke. Because I heard them say my name, of course I thought they were talking about me. The encounter abruptly ended, and I sat up in my bed speechless.

The subject of language became a spiritual topic during the inter-testamental period. The debate suggested answers to an important question. Is there an angelic dialect, and if so, does it bear any resemblance to a single language on Earth? Of all the diverse languages in the world, which one was the superior language spoken by angels?

Celestial language is mentioned at times in the pseudepigrapha, a collection of literary works pertaining to Jewish culture circulating during the times of Jesus and the apostles. While the books themselves do not make it to the cannon of Scripture, the literary works were influential enough to be referenced or discussed by the writers of the New Testament.

As we discussed earlier, the book of *First Enoch* did not make it into the recognized cannon; however, Jude 1:14 cites a part of the work giving us an impression the writers of the New Testament placed a value on its message: *"Now Enoch, the seventh from Adam, prophesied about these men also, saying, 'Behold, the Lord comes with ten thousands of His saints.'"*

Other works read by religious leaders in the Second Temple period contain references to angelic language as its own unique dialect requiring supernatural gifts to understand and speak. In the Testament of Job, not to be confused with the book of Job, the pseudepigraphical writing contains the story of Job's daughters receiving three golden boxes containing "three-stringed girdles" that when worn would "endow you with everything good" (11:14). "For they were not earthly work, but celestial sparks of light flashed through them like the rays of the sun" (11:13). Each daughter placed the girdle around the waist, giving them different supernatural experiences.

The first daughter to wear the gift experienced something very similar to Paul's third heaven experience, *"And I know such a man—whether in the body or out of the body I do not know, God knows—how he was caught up into Paradise and heard inexpressible words, which it is not lawful for a man to utter"* (2 Cor. 12:3–4).

> Then rose the one whose name was Day (Yemima) and girt herself; and immediately she departed her body, as her father had said, and she put on another heart, as if she never cared for earthly things. And she sang angelic hymns in the voice of angels, and she chanted forth the angelic praise of God while dancing.
>
> —Testament of Job 11:23–24[4]

Similar experiences were reported by the other sisters as they wore the gift that gave them the ability to speak in angelic languages. Each of them reported to have lost the desire for worldly things and simultaneously to have been given an ability to communicate in the angelic dialects of heavenly rulers and cherubim (see 11:25–28).

Alternative views were also evidenced in Second Temple literature, crediting the Hebrew language as the designated tongue of the angels. The book of Jubilees contains this idea as it recounts Abraham's story of being called by God, writing,

> And the Lord God said: "Open his mouth and his ears, that he may hear and speak with his mouth, with the language which has been revealed"; for it had ceased from the mouths of all the children of men from the day of the overthrow (of Babel). And I opened his mouth, and his ears and his lips, and I began to speak with him in Hebrew in the tongue of the creation.
>
> —Jubilees 12:25–26[5]

While all these accounts may contain interesting notions on the angelic dialects, it is the scriptural account that carries the authority. Without a doubt, the apostle Paul would have been familiar with all of these different ideas understood by the spiritual leadership of his day. He was a studied Pharisee, *"a Hebrew of the Hebrews"* (Phil. 3:5). He would have been privy to Second Temple Literature, while also keeping *"the righteousness which is in the law, blameless"* (Phil. 3:6). Paul, who wrote much of the New Testament, took a different approach, communicating the tongues of men and the tongues of angels were uniquely in a category of their own.

Paul used the subject of angelic language to illustrate the importance of love when he wrote, *"Though I speak with the tongues of men and of angels, but have not love, I have become sounding brass or a clanging cymbal"* (1 Cor. 13:1). In other words, angelic language without love is nothing more than a gong show.

However, Paul was not an anti-tongue guy. His support for tongues can be heard in his words, *"I thank my God I speak with tongues more than you all"* (1 Cor. 14:18). Paul clearly embraced the power of tongues but showed just how powerless the gift can become if love is not at the center of our practice. While Paul used languages as an example of the dangers of hyper-spirituality, he also emphasized a distinction between the tongues of men and the tongues of angels.

INEXPRESSIBLE WORDS

Paul shed further light on the subject of angelic language when he later revealed a heavenly experience where he heard things that were beyond his ability to communicate within the limits of our language:

> *It is doubtless not profitable for me to boast. I will come to visions and revelations of the Lord: I know a man in Christ who fourteen years ago—whether in the body I do not know, or whether out of the body I do not know, God knows—such a one was caught up to the third heaven. And I know such a man—whether in the body or out of the body I do not know, God knows—how he was caught up into Paradise and heard inexpressible words, which it is not lawful for a man to utter.*
>
> —2 Corinthians 12:1–4

The language barrier became more real than ever before. What Paul heard in the third heaven was beyond anything his mind would comprehend; it could only be identified as *"inexpressible words."* Paul's third heaven experience helps us to understand something about the realm of angels and gives us a clue that angels have a language of their own. Paul could not find the words to articulate the things he heard in the third heaven. Regardless, his experience carried as much validity to him as it would have had he understood everything that was said.

Paul the apostle revealed his third heaven experience in hopes of connecting the Corinthian church to his journey into the apostolic call. It was a moment of great importance to Paul, and he shared this *"in the body or out of the body I do not know"* experience with the church in hopes that they would not just see Paul the man, but Christ in Paul. *"Inexpressible words"* would have conveyed to the reader that where Paul was (in the third heaven) was a place unlike anything ever seen on Earth. Everything was different there and to try to explain what he saw was *"not lawful for a man to utter"* (2 Cor. 2:4). The language was different. The culture was different. Angels and all that were there were different and superior to anything this side of Heaven. It is apparent that Heaven has a culture of its own.

THE CULTURE OF ANGELS

Angels may seem like a minor subject, but the reality is they are big deal partners with God in the invisible world just like you and I are in the natural world. They are as invested in the testimony of Jesus as you and I are. We work on this side of the eternal realm, and they work on the other side of the eternal world. Whether in the unseen realm or the physical world, together, we partner with them to advance the Kingdom of God.

But you have come to Mount Zion and to the city of the living God, the heavenly Jerusalem, to an innumerable company of angels, to the general assembly and church of the firstborn who are registered in heaven, to God the Judge of all, to the spirits of just men made perfect, to Jesus the Mediator of the new covenant, and to the blood of sprinkling that speaks better things than that of Abel.

—Hebrews 12:22–24

When the angel took John through a visionary tour of the Revelation of Jesus Christ, John fell to his knees to worship the angel for the splendor of everything he had been privileged to see. However, the angel stopped John and reassured him that he was not to be worshiped as he was in many ways just like John, and his priorities were the same as the community of believers. The angel was a *"fellow servant"* like John, and his service was alongside the fellowship of those who keep the testimony of Jesus!

And I fell at his feet to worship him. But he said to me, "See that you do not do that! I am your fellow servant, and of your brethren who have the testimony of Jesus. Worship God! For the testimony of Jesus is the spirit of prophecy."

—Revelation 19:10

Just like angels who have what seems like a native language, angels also have food that is regarded as their own. Not to be confused with angel food cake, angel's food is regarded as the bread of Heaven. As the children of Israel wandered in the wilderness, God provided for them and fed to them the food of the angels.

> *Yet He had commanded the clouds above, and opened the doors of heaven, had rained down manna on them to eat, and given them of the bread of heaven. Men ate angels' food; He sent them food to the full.*
>
> —Psalm 78:23–25

As the Israelites' store of food resources became low, God told Moses, *"Behold, I will rain bread from heaven for you. And the people shall go out and gather a certain quota every day . . ."* (Exod. 16:4). When the children of Israel asked Moses what the bread was, they asked in Hebrew *"Ma'n Hu?"* (Exod. 16:5). The angel's food, called the bread of Heaven, was given a name, *"And the house of Israel called its name Manna. And it was like white coriander seed, and the taste of it was like wafers made with honey"* (Exod. 16:31). This tasty new food was given the name manna, which literally means *what.*

The angel's food seems to have some sort of energizing element, granting those who eat it supernatural strength. When the prophet Elijah was given awakened by the Angel of the Lord, he was commanded to eat the food prepared by the Angel. The food had a supernatural effect on him as we are told, *"He went in the strength of that food forty days and forty nights as far as Horeb, the mountain of God"* (1 Kings 19:8).

Maybe you need the same strength for the next portion of the spiritual journey God is calling you to take. Like Elijah, you are promised bread from Heaven, angel's food or manna, to strengthen you as you put your trust in the Lord. Jesus promised, *"He who has an ear, let him hear what the Spirit says to the churches. To him who overcomes I will give some of the hidden manna to eat"* (Rev. 2:17). For those who believe upon Him, Christ has reserved bread from Heaven that no one knows about! God wants to give you angel's food!

There are many other things that we can see from the Word about the culture of angels. Angels seem to travel between Heaven and Earth as revealed in Jacob's dream, showing *"a ladder was set up on the earth, and its top reached to heaven; and there the angels of God were ascending and descending on it"* (Gen. 28:12). What goes up must come down!

At times, angels seem to camp out collectively in a location. As Jacob journeyed to meet his brother, he ran into a camp of angels who seemed to be very welcoming: *"So Jacob went on his way, and the angels of God met him. When Jacob saw them, he said, 'This is God's camp.' And he called the name of that place Mahanaim"* (Gen. 32:1–2). The word *Mahanaim* means "double camp," quite possibly referring to a known place to camp for humans and, to Jacob's surprise, the angels as well!

Angels existed before us and have a history of their own. We may only get small doses of their history as God has reserved quite a bit for us, as it says, *"For now we see in a mirror, dimly, but then face to face. Now I know in part, but then I shall know just as I also am known"* (1 Cor. 13:12). What we do know is that angels do have a culture of their own, a primary language, and food reserved for them that we are invited to eat. The Spirit of God generously calls us to participate in what was previously only available to angels. Whether it is the food of angels or the tongues of angels, God is sharing with us the *secrets of the angels*. Let us explore how we can participate in this mystery?

A NEW TONGUE

We live in a world where the currency of our words is anchored to the natural limits of the human language. There are English words that are difficult to translate into any other language as there are no true equivalents. Words like serendipity have been voted as one of ten English words that are most difficult to translate.[6] I can tell you personally the uneasy feeling I get when I am speaking to a foreign audience at the mercy of the skill of the interpreter. Things get lost in translation. Words lose their currency as multiple words are used to interpret the meaning of one word.

> *For with stammering lips and another tongue He will speak to this people, to whom He said, "This is the rest with which You may cause the weary to rest," and, "This is the refreshing";*
> *yet they would not hear.*
>
> —Isaiah 28:11–12

Language is a powerful form of currency, but language barriers were put in place at Babel to limit man's ability to harness this power. God intentionally slowed down man's ability to get things done by confusing the languages. Communicating in the same language as someone you know can be hard enough. Getting your point across requires skill and timing. This is why King Solomon wrote, *"A word fitly spoken is like apples of gold in settings of silver"* (Prov. 25:11).

The currency of your word depends upon the value it has to connect with others. If the word you speak is received as good as gold, your word is acts like a currency. Job understood this when he lamented,

> *Men listened to me and waited, and kept silence for my*
> *counsel. After my words they did not speak again, and my*
> *speech settled on them as dew. They waited for me as for*
> *the rain, and they opened their mouth wide as for the*
> *spring rain.*
>
> —Job 29:21–23

You may have seen tongues practiced in various ways at churches and other events. Or perhaps you have heard stories of missionaries supernaturally speaking in the indigenous language of the people they have been sent to. There are real accounts of stories like this that shock the mind and confront our understanding of what is possible with God when we minister His Word. However, this tongue is reserved for those who seek an audience with God. Paul writes about this mystery, saying, *"For he who speaks in a tongue does not speak to men but to God, for no one understands him; however, in the spirit he speaks mysteries"* (1 Cor. 14:2).

Words hold value like currency, and God wants to give us a new tongue—a language that has never lost its value, one that has been spoken beyond the edge of time and space before the creation of humanity. This is the *secret of the tongues of angels*. The *secret of the tongues of angels* empowers you to speak directly to God, communing with Him in the spirit over the mysteries of God. It calls us to join in with Heaven's choir and sing as one voice. Perhaps this is what John saw in the ceremony of the scroll when Jesus is found worthy to take the scroll from the hand of the Father and all of Heaven and earth are joining as one to worship.

> *Then I looked, and I heard the voice of many angels around the throne, the living creatures, and the elders; and the number of them was ten thousand times ten thousand, and thousands of thousands, saying with a loud voice: "Worthy is the Lamb who was slain to receive power and riches and wisdom, and strength and honor and glory and blessing!" And every creature which is in heaven and on the earth and under the earth and such as are in the sea, and all that are in them, I heard saying: "Blessing and honor and glory and power be to Him who sits on the throne, and to the Lamb, forever and ever!" Then the four living creatures said, "Amen!" And the twenty-four elders fell down and worshiped Him who lives forever and ever.*
>
> —Revelation 5:11–14

PERFECT SUPERNATURAL STORM

A perfect storm can be defined as "an unusual combination of events or things that produce an unusually bad or powerful result."[7] When a meteorological event converges with a combination of rare circumstances, the effects are of biblical proportions. Pentecost was a perfect storm on a cosmic level.

On the day of Pentecost, the inauguration of the age of the Spirit began. What began with Jesus would now multiply in all who would believe. The gifts of the Spirit that Jesus operated in would now move through all. The Promise of the Spirit would rest upon the believers, giving them the ability to operate in heavenly authority here on Earth. Jesus assured them, *"Behold, I send the Promise of My Father upon you; but tarry in the city of Jerusalem until you are endued with power from on high"* (Luke 24:49).

As the disciples gathered in the upper room to pray *"with one accord in one place,"* a combination of supernatural events converged together in one place forming a perfect supernatural storm:

> *And suddenly there came a sound from heaven, as of a rushing mighty wind, and it filled the whole house where they were sitting. Then there appeared to them divided tongues, as of fire, and one sat upon each of them. And they were all filled with the Holy Spirit and began to speak with other tongues, as the Spirit gave them utterance.*
>
> —Acts 2:2–4

The timing of this event is no coincidence. The feast of Pentecost brought Jews from *"every nation under heaven"* who came to Jerusalem to celebrate the feast (Acts 2:6). The sound that came from Heaven was so loud, it brought them all together to see what was going on.

> *And when this sound occurred, the multitude came together, and were confused, because everyone heard them speak in*

his own language. Then they were all amazed and marveled,
saying to one another, "Look, are not all these who speak
Galileans?"

—Acts 2:6–7

It would be easy to interpret this moment as if the disciples were speaking fluently in all the foreign languages. However, the fifteen different countries notably present at this gathering could hear each of the disciples in their own native language: *"And how is it that we hear, each in our own language in which we were born? . . . We hear them speaking in our own tongues the wonderful works of God"* (Acts 2:8, 11) Each disciple speaking in a tongue could be heard by everyone present in their national language. One tongue to bring them all back and undo what was done at the tower of Babel.

The unlimited power of a unified language was taken from mankind at Babel, and now the Father has reversed the curse at the outpouring of His Spirit. This is the same power that God saw was too much for those at Babel, but He has now restored it to us by His Holy Spirit.

And the Lord said, "Indeed the people are one and they all
have one language, and this is what they begin to do; now
nothing that they propose to do will be withheld from them."

—Genesis 11:6

Not all who were present heard what was being said by the disciples, *"Others mocking said, 'They are full of new wine'"* (Acts 2:13). They were so close to what was happening through the disciples, yet so far

169

away in their hearts that they could not hear it. A similar event took place when the Father spoke audibly from Heaven when Jesus prayed, *"Father, glorify Your name"* (John 12:28). Then the voice from Heaven said, *"I have both glorified it and will glorify it again "* (v. 28). Not all who stood by heard it like John did as he recorded it in his gospel account as some mistakenly thought it was a possible weather-related phenomenon: *"Therefore the people who stood by and heard it said that it had thundered. Others said, 'An angel has spoken to Him'"* (v. 29).

Whether it was the voice of the Father or the disciples speaking in other tongues, Heaven is speaking in a language that can only be heard by those who have ears to hear, eyes to see, and a heart that understands (see Isa. 6:10). God wants to give you the power of this secret. He desires to open your eyes to see the in the unseen realm. He desires to open your ears to hear the tongues of angels.

KEYS TO UNLOCKING THIS SECRET

The *secret of the tongues of angels* is a powerful invitation to join our voice to the angelic voices who are in Heaven. Heaven is speaking and God wants to give you ears to hear the power of this secret.

A HEART TO HEAR

The Scripture attaches heart to language when it speaks about hearing God and seeing what He is revealing. For example, Ezekiel wrote, *"Moreover He said to me: 'Son of Man, receive into your heart all*

My words that I speak to you, and hear with your ears'" (3:10). The ability to take in the riches of God's glory is seen with *"the eyes of your heart"* (Eph. 1:17 ESV). The inability to hear what Heaven is saying stems from a dull heart, as God said, *"Make the heart of this people dull, and their ears heavy"* (Isa. 6:10). God wants to give you a heart to hear what He is saying. Begin by asking Him for a renewed heart! Pray this prayer with me:

Father, I ask You to renew my heart. Let me heart be open to hear everything You are speaking. "Create in me a clean heart, O God, and renew a steadfast spirit within me" (Ps. 51:10). Wash my heart by the manifest presence of Your Spirit. Write Your Word upon my heart, and let me hear You through dreams and visions. Open my eyes and give me ears to hear. In Jesus' name. Amen.

PRAY FOR A FRESH PENTECOST

And it shall come to pass in the last days, says God, That I will pour out of My Spirit on all flesh....

—Acts 2:17

It is time for a fresh outpouring of the Holy Spirit. As the prophet Joel said, *"And it shall come to pass afterward that I will pour out My Spirit on all flesh"* (2:28). The same Spirit who raised Christ from the dead lives in you (see Rom. 8:10)! No single move of God has captured the fullness of Pentecost. There is a fresh Pentecost coming, and it is time to pray for the same power and presence that filled the disciples as they sought the Lord in the upper room.

When they were filled with the Holy Spirit, Heaven and Earth converged in a sound of celestial worship. As those watching said, *"We hear them speaking in our own tongues the wonderful works of God"* (Acts 2:11). Whether you pray in the Spirit or not, pray for a fresh outpouring of the Holy Spirit. It's time for Heaven to once again touch Earth for this generation.

Pray this prayer with me:

Lord Jesus, I ask for the power of the Holy Spirit to flood my heart with the tongues of Heaven. Thank You for your Holy Spirit who helps me in my weakness. Let Heaven's love flow through me like the tongues of angels to beautifully declare the wonders of Your glory! Let my mouth be an instrument of praise. I will worship You with my understanding, and I will worship You with my spirit. Amen.

NOTES

1. Ludwig Wittgenstein, *Tractatus Logico-Philosophicus* (New York: Harcourt, Brace & Company, Inc. 1922).

2. Steven Sande, "Arthur C. Clarke's 2001 Newspad finally arrives, nine years late," engadget, January 28, 2010, https://www.engadget .com/2010-01-28-arthur-c-clarkes-2001-newspad-finally-arrives -nine-years-late.html.

3. "How many languages are there in the world?" *Ethnologue Languages of the World*, https://www.ethnologue.com/guides/how-many -languages.

4. "Testament of Job," trans. M. R. James, rev. Jeremy Kapp, http://gos pel.thruhere.net/BibleStudy/Downloads2/Testament-of-Job-Revised -English.pdf.

5. R. H. Charles, *The Apocrypha and Pseudepigrapha of the Old Testament* (Oxford: Clarendon Press, 1913), "The Book of Jubilees," http://www.pseudepigrapha.com/jubilees/12.htm.

6. "A Short History of the Word 'Serendipity,'" https://interestinglitera ture.com/2015/01/a-short-history-of-the-word-serendipity.

7. *Collins English Dictionary Online*, s.v. "perfect storm," https://www .collinsdictionary.com/dictionary/english/perfect-storm.

CHAPTER 8

THE SECRET OF THE MINISTRY OF ANGELS

*But you have come to Mount Zion and to the city
of the living God, the heavenly Jerusalem,
to an innumerable company of angels.*

—Hebrews 12:22

*There is a set of advantages that have to do with
material resources, and there is a set that have to do
with the absence of material resources—and the reason
underdogs win as often as they do is that the latter is
sometimes every bit the equal of the former.*

—Malcom Gladwell[1]

The feeling of being outnumbered, the one where your head is trying to convince you of the terrible odds against you—that feeling is the enemy's way of convincing you that you are alone, but you are not alone. God is with you, and His angels are with you, giving you the invisible majority. You cannot afford to anchor your faith in what you see, for what you do not see is more powerful than any physical limitation you face.

You are surrounded with an innumerable company of angels, and the enemy knows it. His only tactic is to keep you blind to what he knows gives you the superior advantage. However, God wants to open your eyes to see the realm of the angelic and understand your upper hand. You are not alone.

When the king of Syria could not understand why Israel was not walking into their ambush, he found out it was because Elisha the prophet had a secret weapon. The Syrian king was concerned that his own kingdom had a mole, a man on the inside telling Israel their military plans. However, the king's servants informed him of something more terrifying to his evil plot: *"And one of his servants said, 'None, my lord, O king; but Elisha, the prophet who is in Israel, tells the king of Israel the words that you speak in your bedroom'"* (2 Kings 6:12). The king knew what was required—take out the prophet, and he'd take out Israel.

You see, the enemy is trying to kill the prophetic advantage you have when you hear God and take action on what you hear in the secret place. You have an unseen advantage, and if you know how to use it, you will have victory over every scheme of the enemy.

When the king of Syria moved to destroy the prophet, he had an army equipped with horses and chariots sent to deal with him. When Elisha was awakened by his servant to the terrifying news of the heavily equipped army, the servant had already done the math. They were outnumbered. However, Elisha was not convinced because his eyes were not looking in the natural, for his advantage was in the supernatural.

So he answered, "Do not fear, for those who are with us are more than those who are with them." And Elisha prayed, and said, "Lord, I pray, open his eyes that he may see." Then the Lord opened the eyes of the young man, and he saw. And behold, the mountain was full of horses and chariots of fire all around Elisha. So when the Syrians came down to him, Elisha prayed to the Lord, and said, "Strike this people, I pray, with blindness." And He struck them with blindness according to the word of Elisha.

—2 Kings 6:16–18

God wants to open your eyes to see. He wants to give you an ability to see in the unseen realm and partner with the angelic forces of Heaven to experience total victory. God has sent His angels to accomplish His purpose, and now is the time to put fear away and open your eyes to God's special forces on assignment.

ANGELS ON ASSIGNMENT

One of the questions I am often asked about angels is, "Why angels? Why doesn't Jesus just do it Himself?" That is a good question, but it clearly represents our ignorance of the way the Kingdom operates. To think that a king would do it all himself is like expecting the founder of Starbucks to personally craft your latte. Why would he do that when he has plenty of trained staff to do that for you? Angels have delegated assignments because Jesus is King. The King's job is not running around and micromanaging His Kingdom. Let's be clear, the King's place is on His throne, and no angel can sit there!

SECRETS OF THE ANGELS

But to which of the angels has He ever said: "Sit at My right hand, till I make Your enemies Your footstool"? Are they not all ministering spirits sent forth to minister for those who will inherit salvation?

—Hebrews 1:13–14

The King is on His throne, and a specially trained staff of angelic forces are diligently at work, ministering to those who are inheriting the Kingdom. You and I have angels assigned to us to administrate the cosmic transfer of the Kingdom of Heaven to the whole Earth. For this cosmic shift to happen, it is vital we learn how to partner with the ministry of angels. Like Elisha's servant, God is going to open our eyes to identify with the innumerable company of angelic forces that have been sent to eliminate every threat. This is the *secret of the ministry of angels*.

SIGNS OF CELESTIAL ACTIVITY

Often times, people will come to me and say, "I cannot see angels." My answer to them is always the same, "Yes, you can. You just do not know what to look for." God wants to give us eyes to see. However, seeing and looking are two different things. You can be watching a movie on the big screen at the local cinema, and as captivated you may be by the enormity of the screen, you still choose what to look at during the film.

Have you ever sat through a movie with a group of friends, and for some reason the one sitting next to you keeps asking, "What just happened? What did he say?" You may be seeing the movie for the first time, but you feel like the involuntary tour guide for the newest Marvel movie. My encouragement to them is the same to you, pay attention! To do that, you are going to need to know what to look for. What are the signs of celestial activity?

When members of the unseen world involve themselves in anything pertaining to the physical world, there are clues given, and they're called signs and wonders. These signs and wonders are demonstrations of the unseen world having an immediate effect on the natural world. The New Testament believers understood the impact that the unseen world had on the natural world. When angels moved out of the unseen realm of Heaven into the natural realm of Earth, the physical world showed signs of celestial activity.

In 2007, I had an encounter that called me into ministry. On the August 24, 2007, I was taken into a prophetic experience where I saw the angel Gabriel. When I write that I saw him, it was not in my spirit or my mind's eye, but I was there in the spirit, where he was. As Paul the apostle wrote concerning his heavenly encounter, *"Whether in the body or out of the body I do not know, God knows,"* the same was very true with this prophetic experience (2 Cor. 12:2).

Two months before, I had a dream foreshadowing this event. I did not know what to expect, but the dream spoke to me that something important was coming. In the dream, I saw an outline of the Lord standing in a doorway speaking to me. He spoke, "I am coming in the month of August, at the time of two-thirds." The dream ended. I could not make sense of it at the time, but I expected breakthrough in August.

I remember what Gabriel looked like. His hair was both black and gold, and his skin was made of gold and silver. His nose was longer in its definition, and he had clouds at his feet. His eyes were deep, and he had the look of a focused man. I was stunned as I stared at him. I fell near his feet and deliberately raised my hands up and began to worship the name of Jesus Christ.

Gabriel spoke something personal, but his very appearance was incredibly significant for the U.S. And that night was the first time it had poured a heavy rain in Nashville, Tennessee, almost all summer.

The following day, I told a good friend and intercessor about the visitation and the rains, and he responded with something very interesting. He spoke with his wife a few days earlier, confirming my visitation with Gabriel. My friend felt like the only thing that could have the potential to break off the drought of Tennessee and the rest of the South would call for Jesus to specifically send the angel Gabriel.

I knew Jesus had sent him to bring rain, and on September 8, a tropical cyclone named "Gabrielle" started heading toward North Carolina. The storm's name was the feminine form of "Gabriel."

When strong angels move into Earth's atmosphere, physical elements begin to shift. Seismic activity, forceful winds, and other signs can begin to tell us that an angel has come into Earth's atmosphere. This is not to suggest that every time an environmental phenomenon occurs it is because of an angel. However, the Scripture illustrates examples of this spiritual-physical reality.

THE ANGEL COMING DOWN & THE EARTHQUAKE

At the tomb of Jesus, when an angel of the Lord came from Heaven *"and rolled back the stone from the door,"* *"there was a great earthquake"* (Matt. 28:2–3). When an angel descends from Heaven, it is felt throughout the region. A great earthquake shakes the ground as a spiritual being makes contact with the physical world. When the disciples were filled again with the Holy Spirit, *"the place where they assembled together was shaken; and they were filled with the Holy Spirit"* (Acts 4:31).

THE SHAKING OF THE MULBERRY TREES

Second Samuel 5:23–25 reads:

> *Therefore David inquired of the Lord, and He said, "You shall not go up; circle around behind them, and come upon them in front of the mulberry trees. And it shall be, when you hear the sound of marching in the tops of the mulberry trees, then you shall advance quickly. For then the Lord will go out before you to strike the camp of the Philistines." And David did so, as the Lord commanded him; and he drove back the Philistines from Geba as far as Gezer.*

While the text does not indicate the direct involvement of angels, we can only imagine what was taking place in the unseen world. What is the indicator that the Lord is going out to battle with David? He is instructed to listen for the *"sound of marching in the tops of the mulberry trees"* (v. 24). It may have been a strong wind sent by God to shake the leaves of the mulberry trees, and that would seem plausible. However, the sound of wind is the first effect described as the indicator

181

of heavenly activity when the disciples gathered for the outpouring of the Spirit on the day of Pentecost (see Acts 2:2).

THE ANGEL & THE STIRRING OF THE WATER

I love the story in John 5 about the stirring of the water because it ends with a miracle given to a man who could not get down to the water fast enough for his healing.

> *Now there is in Jerusalem by the Sheep Gate a pool, which is called in Hebrew, Bethesda, having five porches. In these lay a great multitude of sick people, blind, lame, paralyzed, waiting for the moving of the water. For an angel went down at a certain time into the pool and stirred up the water; then whoever stepped in first, after the stirring of the water, was made well of whatever disease he had.*
>
> —John 5:2–4

In verse six, Jesus asked the man, *"Do you want to be made well?"*

"Sir, I have no man to put me into the pool when the water is stirred up; but while I am coming, another steps down before me," he told Jesus (v. 7).

Jesus did not try to rationalize with the man about his situation or give him a new strategy to beat everyone else into the water at the next angelic event. Instead, Jesus commanded the man, *"Rise, take up your bed and walk"* (v. 8). In that moment, the man jumped to his feet, picked up his bed, and walked!

Up until Jesus' appearance, the sick and the lame would wait for the stirring of the water. If this were simply superstition as some suggest, there would not be a history of healing at that place. The text tells us an angel would stir the water, and whoever stepped in first *"was made well of whatever disease he had"* (v. 4). This was not a trick, and these people were not simply psyching themselves up! This was known as a place of healing as the angel stirred the water. However, when the Healer shows up at this place, He only had to speak healing over the sick and the lame. He did not need water to assist Him because Jesus is the living water (Jer. 2:13; John 4:10)!

PRAYER ACTIVATES THE MINISTRY OF ANGELS

Prayer that connects with God activates the realm of angels. They await His word and are then sent forth to minister His will. This is what King Hezekiah did with the help of Isaiah the prophet as they called on Heaven to intervene in their struggle with an enemy king:

Now because of this King Hezekiah and the prophet Isaiah, the son of Amoz, prayed and cried out to heaven. Then the Lord sent an angel who cut down every mighty man of valor, leader, and captain in the camp of the king of Assyria. So he returned shamefaced to his own land. And when he had gone into the temple of his god, some of his own offspring struck him down with the sword there.

—2 Chronicles 32:20–21

It is so important that we learn to pray. Out of all the things Jesus taught His disciples, the one specific thing the disciples asked Jesus to teach them was how to pray (see Luke 11:1). In Luke 10, Jesus sent out the seventy to bring healing and the good news of the Kingdom of Heaven. However, when they returned, they realized something was different. Yes, they had seen miracles and done amazing works, but they had seen Jesus do it with such ease. What was the difference? They realized it was Jesus' prayer life. So, they asked Him, *"Teach us to pray"* (Luke 11:1). He instructed them:

> *So He said to them, "When you pray, say: Our Father in heaven, Hallowed be Your name. Your kingdom come. Your will be done on earth as it is in heaven. Give us day by day our daily bread. And forgive us our sins, for we also forgive everyone who is indebted to us. And do not lead us into temptation, but deliver us from the evil one."*
>
> —Luke 11:2–4

The "Our Father" prayer is not a mantra; it is a mission to bring Heaven to Earth, and Jesus wants us to pray with expectation that Heaven is going to invade everything everywhere. As someone once said, "What goes up must come down," and when we look up and pray, Heaven comes down to stay. How do we pray when we don't know what to pray? We pray the Word!

WORDS AND WORKS

Psalm 103:20 tells us that angels *"do His word, heeding the voice of His word."* Bill Johnson in *When Heaven Invades Earth* explained what happens when people of God speak the words of God:

Angels await the people of God speaking His word. I believe angels pick up the fragrance of the throne room through the word spoken by people. They can tell when a word has its origins in the heart of the Father. And, in turn, they recognize that word as their assignment.

How can you partner with the ministry of angels? Well, the most powerful thing in the universe is the spoken Word of God, and He has commissioned you to give His Word a voice! The visible world was framed by an invisible God who speaks words that are capable of forming physical matter. God has given us His Word, but that does not mean He has stopped talking—how could He when His name is called *"The Word"* (John 1:1)!

The promise of the power of His word is activated when we operate in faith. Jesus gave us this promise. When the disciples stood stunned by the effect of Jesus' word on the withered fig tree, they marveled and said, *"How did the fig tree wither away so soon?"* (Mark. 21:20). The moment Jesus spoke to the fig tree, *"Let no fruit grow on you ever again,"* the power of His invisible word caused an immediate effect on physical matter (v. 19). The disciples could not help themselves. How did He do it?

> *So Jesus answered and said to them, "Assuredly, I say to you, if you have faith and do not doubt, you will not only do what was done to the fig tree, but also if you say to this mountain, 'Be removed and be cast into the sea,' it will be done. And whatever things you ask in prayer, believing, you will receive."*
>
> —Matthew 21:21–22

All matter was created by the word of God, and when paired with faith, words can move matter. Jesus uses the moving of a mountain by speaking in faith as an example of prayer. However, what kind of prayer looks like speaking to a mountain? I thought prayer is speaking directly to God, right? Well, let me show you something that illustrates this principle clearly.

In the middle of a great battle, Joshua the successor to Moses, led the children of Israel to an incredible victory. Israel faced overwhelming odds; ten kings had banded together to fight Joshua and his mighty men of valor. However, God was with Joshua, and with the Lord of hosts fighting for him, Joshua had the majority. How did Joshua partner with God's plan in that moment? He spoke to the hosts of Heaven: the sun, moon, and stars.

> *Then Joshua spoke to the Lord in the day when the Lord delivered up the Amorites before the children of Israel, and he said in the sight of Israel: "Sun, stand still over Gibeon; and Moon, in the Valley of Aijalon." So the sun stood still, and the moon stopped, till the people had revenge upon their enemies. Is this not written in the Book of Jasher? So the sun stood still in the midst of heaven, and did not hasten to go down for about a whole day. And there has been no day like that, before it or after it, that the Lord heeded the voice of a man; for the Lord fought for Israel.*
>
> —Joshua 10:12–14

The writer connected Joshua's speaking to the celestial lights with *"the Lord heeded the voice of a man"* (v. 14). The writer was trying to make it clear that Joshua had spoken it, but God was the One who actually made it happen. This is the principle of speaking God's word.

In August of 2014, I was spending some time ministering in Sonoma County, California. I had just returned to the hotel from a meeting that Saturday night and was looking forward to the next morning's Sunday service. At about 3:18 a.m., I woke up out of bed into a vision, and at the same time, I waspraying a prayer as I was watching what I was shown. I began boldly declaring this prayer as I watched in a vision the archangel Michael fighting against satan. As they fought, Michael began to say to the devil, "The Lord rebuke you!"

At that moment I remembered in Jude 1:9 how Michael the archangel fought against the devil over the body of Moses and spoke the same thing at that time, *"The Lord rebuke you!"* (Jude 1:9). So, I too began declaring the written Word and what I was seeing, saying out loud, "Lord, rebuke the enemy! Lord, rebuke the enemy!" I kept saying it as I wrestled through what I was watching in the vision. I was speaking what I saw in God's Word and watching it unfold before me in the unseen realm!

As the clock turned to 3:20 a.m., the door began to shake, and it seemed like the room was shaking as well. Even more boldly, I kept praying, "Lord, rebuke the enemy!" Suddenly, I realized my bed was wildly shaking and car alarms started going off outside in every direction. My assistant who had traveled with me for this trip woke up and calmly said, "It's an earthquake," as if he had been in one before. I continued to pray as everything began to calm. By now, everyone you could think of was outside trying to regroup. I just watched stunned by what had just happened. Something in the spiritual realm had just

187

taken place, and I knew there would be more to uncover as the weekend progressed.

The next morning, I sat with my coffee and watched the local morning news. Everyone in the hotel was silent, listening to the report of the earthquake and its damage. At first, they recorded the magnitude of the quake as 6.1 but changed it later that morning and confirmed it as a 6.0, which at that date was the largest earthquake to hit California's Napa Valley in twenty-five years.[2]

Although there were few injuries for the size of the earthquake we experienced, the things most effected were barrels and bottles of wine. It was reported that the cost of damages could have topped one billion dollars.[3] The principal core affected by the earthquake was the wine industry. Wine bottles and barrels rolled off the shelves, allowing the wine to escape its containers. What is even more wild was the wine that had burst out of the barrels and bottles was reported to have been running through the streets in small streams. God was speaking, and I was paying attention!

> *"Behold, the days are coming," says the Lord, "When the plowman shall overtake the reaper, and the treader of grapes him who sows seed; the mountains shall drip with sweet wine, and all the hills shall flow with it."*
>
> —Amos 9:13

That Sunday was wild at church. Everyone was buzzing with what had happened in the night. While everyone wondered what this all meant, I knew because I was watching, waiting, praying, and speaking God's

Word! I got a front row seat to what was taking place in the unseen realm! The angels of God were in a battle with the enemy who had a stronghold over that region. God was dealing with that spiritual force of wickedness, and we felt it!

Now, let me give some thoughts on what I believed happened in this supernatural and physical shaking. What happened in the natural was a sign of what the armies of Heaven were doing to shake the enemy's grip off of that state. The wine that ran through down the streets of Sonoma County, California, was a sign of what God was releasing as a result of the shaking. It is time for new wine! It's the wine of God's Spirit poured out for all, no longer held back for another time! The Spirit of the Lord is ready to move and fill the highways and byways. What happened in the spirit realm was experienced in the physical.

Now is the time to speak God's word! Now is the time for those who will keep the watch of the Lord and speak His word to activate the realm of the angels into action! This is the *secret of the ministry of angels*. God has placed His word in your mouth! Do not hesitate to speak it when He is moving on you! The *secret of the ministry of angels* is that you and I get to participate in giving God's word a voice.

WAIT, WATCH, & SAY

The prophet Habakkuk demonstrated this secret when he wrote, *"I will stand my watch . . . to see what He will say to me, and what I will answer when I am corrected"* (2:1). Did you catch that? He not only watched to see what God would say, Habakkuk also watched to see what He would say in response. He knew the only wise thing that could be said by his mouth was going to have to come from God. Habakkuk's partnership with God's word, not only to listen, but also to speak, was the prophetic call upon his life.

Ezekiel had the same experience when he was carried away in the Spirit to a valley of dry bones: *"Son of man, can these bones live,"* the Lord asked Ezekiel. *"Only you know, Oh Lord God, You know,"* responded Ezekiel (Ezek. 37:3). Ezekiel was a smart prophet. He knew not to presume anything in the presence of God. Only God can answer His own questions!

God spoke again to Ezekiel, giving him the words to speak as an answer to His question, *"Prophesy to these bones, and say to them, 'O dry bones, hear the word of the Lord!'"* (Ezek. 37:4). Then we read:

> *So I prophesied as I was commanded; and as I prophesied, there was a noise, and suddenly a rattling; and the bones came together, bone to bone. Indeed, as I looked, the sinews and the flesh came upon them, and the skin covered them over; but there was no breath in them. Also He said to me, "Prophesy to the breath, prophesy, son of man, and say to the breath, 'Thus says the Lord God: "Come from the four winds, O breath, and breathe on these slain, that they may live."'" So I prophesied as He commanded me, and breath came into them, and they lived, and stood upon their feet, an exceedingly great army.*
>
> —Ezekiel 37:7–10

The *secret of the ministry of angels* operates by this same principle. Watch to speak what God is saying. Keeping the watch of the Lord is not meant to simply be an exercise in stillness. The watch of the Lord is sitting at the feet of the King until He speaks, and when He does, He will instruct us as to what to say! Let's dive deeper into what this looks like.

SPEAKING IN SYNC

At the Revelation of Jesus, John received the call to come up into the heavenly realm and see a panorama of future events. The voice he heard, was the voice of Jesus. However, the voice was not just speaking to John or at John; the voice is seen speaking with John.

> *After these things I looked, and behold, a door standing open in heaven. And the first voice which I heard was like a trumpet speaking with me, saying, "Come up here, and I will show you things which must take place after this."*
>
> —Revelation 4:1

When we carefully read the text, we discover there was only one person speaking. John, however, was not an idle observer of what was happening. John was speaking with the Voice while the Voice was speaking with him. They were in sync. John was in simultaneous synchronization with the Voice, and there was no delay between what God was speaking and what John was repeating.

They say identical twins often finish each other's sentences. Well, John was so in sync with the Lord that he was not just twinning; he was joined to the Lord in such a way that he was in complete sync with what God was saying. He was one spirit with the Lord: *"But he who is joined to the Lord is one spirit with Him"* (1 Cor. 6:17).

God wants to bring you into such a synchronization with His Spirit that there is no disconnect between what He is speaking and what you are saying. You may hear the word in the spirit, but when you speak the word out loud in the physical world, you are becoming a voice for God's word. The *secret of the ministry of angels* empowers us to be a participant in the things of Heaven on this earth. While angels are like the air force, you and I are like the ground force. Our communications with each other are transmitted by the spoken word of God. When we come into sync with the word of God, we invite everything in Heaven into the atmosphere of Earth. When we pair our voice to the word of God, we create an atmosphere for Heaven to effect Earth. The *secret of the ministry of angels* gives us the power of partnership to speak God's word so that angels can do what God is saying.

KEYS TO UNLOCKING THIS SECRET

The *secret of the ministry of angels* is a powerful invitation to partner with angels in the administration of God's word. Angels are waiting for you to speak the word, and as you do, they are hearing the voice of God move through you, giving them permission to do what God is saying!

THE WORD HELPS YOU TO SEE

The first key to understanding how to partner with the ministry of angels is understanding that the Word of God helps you to see the unseen things. But, how do we hear the Word of God? We must understand the Word of God can be heard in two different ways: the written Word and the spoken word. This is known as the *logos* and the *rhema*. The *logos* is the declared written Word while the *rhema* refers to the spoken word. Knowing the written Word gives you an advantage to hear the spoken word.

When Jesus walked with the two travelers on the road to Emmaus, He spoke *rhema* to them from the *logos* of the Scriptures: *"And beginning at Moses and all the Prophets, He expounded to them in all the Scriptures the things concerning Himself"* (Luke 24:27). However, they could not tell it was Jesus at first because their *"eyes were restrained, so that they did not know Him"* (v. 16). Just because they could look at Him, does not mean they could see Him. He broke bread with them, and their eyes were opened to see Jesus and know it was Him (see vv. 30–31). Their response to the moment they recognized it was Jesus is a perfect example of the *logos* becoming *rhema*: *"And they said to one another, "Did not our heart burn within us while He talked with us on the road, and while He opened the Scriptures to us?"* (v. 32). The *logos* and the *rhema* were working on their hearts to really see.

The first key to understanding how to partner with the ministry of angels is understanding that angels partner with the Word of God. The Word helps you to see what has been previously hidden in plain sight. The psalmist would say it this way, *"Your word is a lamp to my feet and a light to my path"* (Ps. 119:105). The Word of God illuminates your vision, giving you an ability to see the hidden things. As you carry the Word in your heart, you are going to be more attuned to the things of Heaven.

The Word is going to give you a sensitivity to the angelic activity happening around you, and as you speak the Word, angels are released to perform His Word and the voice of His Word (see Ps. 103:20). Give the Word that you are hearing a voice! If you have ever been in a moment while reading the Scriptures and something jumped out at you and stirred your heart, that was the moment a *rhema* word was being released into your spirit. At that moment, speak the word. Start to declare it, and watch Heaven move in!

BE STILL AND KNOW

In *Secrets of the Seer*, I outlined ten keys to activating the seer nature. One of the principal practices that I have found to be a key that increases our ability to hear and see what God is saying is the secret of stillness: *"Be still, and know that I am God; I will be exalted among the nations, I will be exalted in the earth!"* (Ps. 46:10). Those who know how to practice this secret quietly turn off the outside noise of this world so they can open their eyes and ears to the invisible world of the Kingdom. There is a moment in prayer where you feel the holy hush of God, and it draws you into a place of stillness and surrender. It is in this place where we become quiet enough to hear the still small voice of God.

The moments after you receive a *rhema* word are extremely important. At such times, you can begin to declare the word and give the word a voice so that all of creation can hear. At that moment, do not just move on into other things and the busy schedule of life. That is the moment you want to be still in the presence of God and intently watch what you are seeing and receiving from the Spirit of God. In those moments, I yield to the stillness. It is not something I force on myself, but it's something I yield to.

When this happens to you, pay attention! What you are about to sense, see, and know is important. What you see, write down! Capture it and take every thought captive (see 2 Cor. 10:5). When something in the natural world occurs that mirrors what you have seen in these moments of stillness, you can begin to identify what Heaven is doing in the earth. The more of these moments that you observe with the Holy Spirit, the more your eyes are going to accurately see the ministry of angels in everyday situations.

Pray this prayer with me:

Father, I will be still and know that You are God. Let my spirit-man become finely tuned to the realm of Your Holy Spirit. Let my eyes and ears be awakened to the ministry of angels. Open my heart to be in sync with Your voice! What You say, I will say that the angels of God may carry out every word spoken by your Spirit. Amen.

NOTES

1. Malcolm Gladwell, *David and Goliath: Underdogs, Misfits, and the Art of Battling Giants* (New York: Little, Brown and Company, 2013.

2. Max Ehrenfreund, "Why the Napa Valley Earthquake Is Unlikely to Affect Wine Prices," *The Washington Post*, August 25, 2014, https://www.washingtonpost.com/news/wonk/wp/2014/08/25/why-the-napa-valley-earthquake-is-unlikely-to-affect-wine-prices.

3. Maya Rhodan, "Damage from California Earthquake Could Top $1 Billion," Time, August 25, 2014, https://time.com/3173406/california-napa-earthquake-damage.

CONCLUSION

As I finish writing *Secrets of the Angels,* an awe of the greatness of God fills my spirit-man. I am aware that we are only scratching the surface of a very great mystery; however, the secret most cherished and protected by cherubim, seraphim, archangels, and other heavenly beings is the mystery of God's glory. There isn't an angel in Heaven, on Earth, or under the earth who will not bow at the name above all names, Jesus, the Son of the Father, for He is *"the brightness of His glory"* (Heb. 1:3). Angels behold His glory, and my hope is that as we explored the subject of angels, we too entered into the same awe of God that angels experience throughout eternity.

As you have read through the chapters of this book, I hope you continue to explore this fascinating subject with the help of the Holy Spirit. Our understanding of the mysteries of the unseen realm is influenced by the limits of this current age. As the apostle Paul wrote, *"For now we see in a mirror, dimly, but then face to face. Now I know in part, but then I shall know just as I also am known"* (1 Cor. 13:12). And in another place, Paul wrote,

> *But as it is written: "Eye has not seen, nor ear heard, nor have entered into the heart of man the things which God has prepared for those who love Him."*
>
> —1 Corinthians 2:9

SECRETS OF THE ANGELS

The good news is that God wants to show us these mysteries and give us glimpses of what awaits us on the other side of the veil. And we have this promise pertaining to the unseen riches in Christ: *"But God has revealed them to us through His Spirit. For the Spirit searches all things, yes, the deep things of God"* (1 Cor 2:10). Let's recap what we have covered.

In the first chapter, we learned that angels are God's invisible messengers. Angels carry out God's Word and are assigned to watch and protect you as you carry out your God-given purpose. However, the second and third chapters reveal the complicated history of members of the angelic realm. Just as humans have fallen from our fealty to the Creator, so did various members of the angelic race. In doing so, the divine order set forth by YHWH was thrown into chaos, but there is an answer to the disorder, and it is the "Seed," the promised Messiah, Jesus. He would crush the head of the serpent and ultimately restore the Edenic vision.

The secret of the giants contains a clear identification of the monster children of this rebellion and gives language to the enemies you and I face today and the nature of their "seed." The fallen angelic rebels had a vision to populate the earth with their progeny and through them claim the earth as their own. The vision of the Kingdom of God is to dismantle their demonic agenda, and as followers of Jesus, we are to do what Jesus did because we have His "Seed" in us.

> *He who sins is of the devil, for the devil has sinned from the beginning. For this purpose the Son of God was manifested, that He might destroy the works of the devil. Whoever has been born of God does not sin, for His seed remains in him; and he cannot sin, because he has been born of God.*
>
> —1 John 3:8–9

When will all this be completed? The Scriptures assure us of their completion at the appointed time.

> *For the vision is yet for an appointed time; but at the end it*
> *will speak, and it will not lie. Though it tarries, wait for it;*
> *because it will surely come, it will not tarry.*
>
> —Habakkuk 2:3

The secret of the cherubim gives us language to understand God is the sovereign Administrator over all time. Every timeline is in His authority, and the cherubim are His cosmic assistants who attend to the Creator as He navigates time. God wants you to redeem time! Partner with Him to see His purpose accomplished through times and seasons and reverse the curse.

In chapter 5, we explored the seraphim who are stationed as throne guardians of the secret place of God's presence. In Isaiah's vision, we saw them covering their faces with two of their six wings while they attended to God's throne (Isa. 6:2) However, in the Revelation given to the apostle John, they are no longer covering their faces but worshiping before the throne with unveiled faces. Each of their faces are distinct in nature. And like the seraphim, when we worship in Spirit and Truth, the veil is lifted and we behold His glory with unveiled faces.

> *But we all, with unveiled face, beholding as in a mirror the*
> *glory of the Lord, are being transformed into the same image*
> *from glory to glory, just as by the Spirit of the Lord.*
>
> —2 Corinthians 3:18

Archangels are the highest rank of angelic beings. While their rebellious counterparts are identified as principalities, archangels like
Michael and Gabriel are faithful and loyal to their original assignment
and are seen throughout Scripture helping to prepare God's people
for the Messianic purpose of Jesus. There is a war taking place in the
unseen realm. The secret of the archangels explores the tug of war we
participate in as we pray and pull down strongholds. Our prayers pull
on the realm of the supernatural and trigger a chain of supernatural
events in the invisible realm.

However, sometimes we do not know what to pray for, and the Spirit
helps with a language of prayer that breaks through invisible barriers.
The currency of language has been limited by God when He confused
the languages at Babel, thus limiting man's ability to harness the
advantages of a unified language.

The secret of the tongues of angels reveals the power of Pentecost
when the Holy Spirit broke the language barrier off God's people. The
secret of the tongues of angels connects us to the community of angels
and saints in the heavens and gives us the ability to pray as one unified
voice. The power of a unified language was stripped away at Babel,
but the Father has reversed the curse for us when the Holy Spirit was
poured out on Pentecost. This is the same power that God saw was unfit
for those at Babel, but He has now restored it to us by His Holy Spirit.

*And the Lord said, "Indeed the people are one and they all
have one language, and this is what they begin to do; now
nothing that they propose to do will be withheld from them."*
—Genesis 11:6

And finally, the secret of the ministry of angels is a promise given to us as an assurance from God that we are cared for by Him when He sends His angels to minister to us. The promise to us is sure, *"For He shall give His angels charge over you, to keep you in all your ways"* (Ps. 91:11). Even our Lord Jesus received the ministry of angels during and after the devil's onslaught of temptation in wilderness (see Matt. 4:11; Mark 1:13). Before His hour of betrayal, Jesus prayed for the strength to endure the enormity of what was at hand, and we are told, *"Then an angel appeared to Him from heaven, strengthening Him"* (Luke 22:43).

Angels are assigned to minister to you and minister alongside of you as you carry out your Kingdom purpose. God has called you to speak His word and declare His works! Angels carry out His word, and as you give your voice to speak His word, you are partnering with Heaven's messengers to see God's word made manifest. This is the secret of the ministry of angels. God has assigned angels to work together with His saints for the advancement of the Kingdom of God on Earth. Get ready for Heaven and Earth to truly work together to bring about the glory of the great end-time harvest

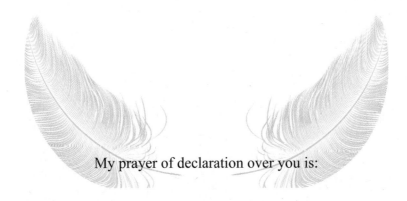

My prayer of declaration over you is:

May the Lord of hosts, the God of the angel armies, open your eyes to see there are more with you than against you. May the Lord cause His angels to surround you and keep you from harm. May the Lord take action against the wicked agenda of principalities and powers who mean you harm and cause them to fall like lightning while their plans come to nothing. May the Lord commission His angels to watch over you in the day and to guard you in the night. May the Lord's plans cause you to prosper and may He send angels to go before you as you step into the land He has promised. May the Lord send you with the support of angels to carry out His Kingdom purpose and may He cause miracles to flow through your life as a demonstration of God's power and love. Amen.

ABOUT JAMIE GALLOWAY

Jamie Galloway carries a revival message that imparts a lifestyle of the supernatural. He has a broad ministry experience from planting churches to speaking at stadium events. He is a sought after prophetic communicator and is involved in various media projects that highlight the move of God for our generation.

SECRETS
OF THE *Seer*
E-COURSE

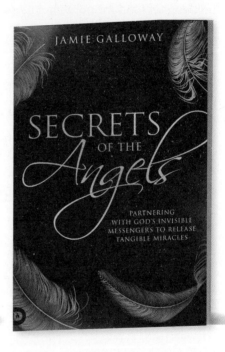

DIVE DEEPER INTO ACTIVATING A SEER LIFESTYLE

Let Jamie take you step-by-step through an exploration of the Ten Secrets in this user friendly online E-Course. Join others and jump into an online learning experience designed to activate a lifestyle of Seer Encounters. Also, enjoy a free message on Heavenly encounters at the web link below.

jamiegalloway.com/secrets